The **Jobhunting Toolkit**
To find the **PERFECT JOB** in tough times

TO KARLA,

THANK YOU FOR YOUR

INVALUABLE CONTRIBUTION!

HOPE YOU ENJOY THE
BOOK

YOURS

Oi Brult

XXXXX

The Jobhunting TOOLKIT

To find the
PERFECT JOB in tough times

Oni Bhattacharya

The **Jobhunting Toolkit**
To find the **PERFECT JOB** in tough times

First published in 2015 by
Panoma Press Ltd
48 St Vincent Drive, St Albans, Herts, AL1 5SJ UK

info@panomapress.com
www.panomapress.com

Cover design by Michael Inns
Artwork by Karen Gladwell

ISBN 978-1-909623-83-5

Contents

	Introduction	*vii*
1	The Myth About There Being No Jobs	1
2	Seven Steps to Find What You Want and Plan How to Get It	5
3	Barriers, Motivation and Changing Your Story: How to Break the Habits of a Lifetime and Get Working	17
4	Where to Look for Work and Make Opportunities Happen	31
5	Applying for Jobs: Rules for Covering Letters, CVs and Application Forms	43
6	How to Get Yourself Noticed by Employers: Direct Methods of Applying for Jobs	69
7	Interview Techniques and What Employers Want	75
8	To Be Hired or Not To Be Hired? That is the Question	109

9 You're Hired, Now Prove You're the Right   119
Person for the Job

10 Do Something Different: 125
Retraining for the Future

11 Creating a Job for Yourself   131

12 Working in the 21st Century   139

13 Getting a Job: Take Action, The Power   153
is in Your Hands

The Final Word   *157*

About the Author   *159*

Introduction

Are you serious about finding work? I mean really serious? I know that it's supposed to be tough out there but there are jobs, despite what everybody says. Most young people have only lived through the good times and know nothing about the bad.

After years of growth and free spending many economies in the western world are said to be in recession. Money is tight and jobs are hard to get. Everyone it seems is pulling in their belts and there is an air of austerity. People are frightened about their future, employers are axing jobs and there are cuts left right and centre.

Having a full-time job is a premium. You are one of the lucky ones – or so it seems. I'm not a believer in the recession theory. I see it just as an adjustment of the economy, especially here in the UK. Gone are the days of loads of money and throwing cash around. Jobs are tougher to find and those being put out of work or trying to find a job are in stiff competition with many others seeking similar positions.

In today's world it really is a jungle out there, and finding the right position requires different thinking from that of the past. You can't just rely on having a job for life; those days are gone. Now you might have to do two or three different jobs to make up for one larger job. The words part-time and flexible are now keys to the future.

There are jobs out there. If you've had trouble finding work, it might have something to do with the way you sell yourself to employers. These days they aren't just hiring anybody. They now put new hoops and barriers in place to exclude people from the process. Even if you do get an interview, you are up against stiff competition.

In essence, you need to be firing on all cylinders and giving it your all to find employment. The reality is that many people simply aren't doing that. They're firing off lame CVs and poor covering letters and then messing up at interview. Others give up and just don't get replies and sink into hopelessness.

How do I know this? For the past four years I've worked as an employability trainer and helped many get back into work. I've seen them shift from being desperate individuals to starting to believe in themselves again and finding jobs. In the end this has nothing to do with me. It's all about you. Yes – YOU!

Everything to do with your life and being employed is down to you. What you want to do? How much you want to work? What you are prepared to do to get a job? How much effort are you are willing to put in to get employed?

I often hear people moan that they haven't got the right qualifications, or use the same reasons. "I have no work experience." "I'm too old." "I'm qualified but nobody will hire me." "If only I had my time again." When I write it down it all seems so lame. They are just excuses and not reasons. Too many people think the world owes them a living; it doesn't. If you want success you have to strive for it. You get nothing just hoping it will happen or expecting it will just come along. It won't; you have to make it happen.

Where you are today, whether employed or not, is down to decisions and choices you made in the past. If you had done things differently you would be on a different path or in a different place. If you're struggling to find work and are not getting interviews, you need to change the way you do things. You need to be clear about what you want and then start working towards it.

Many people are so random in the hunt for work they're simply missing the mark. The lack of focus results in firing off CVs randomly without a hope in hell of getting the job. When they don't get an interview or a reply they think the world is against them. Is this striking a chord with you?

My advice for now is to stop sending CVs and to take stock of where you are now. If you are serious about finding a job you're in the right place. Read on.

In this book I will show you:

- ✓ *Despite what they say, there are jobs out there.*
- ✓ *How to focus on what you want and then move towards it.*
- ✓ *How to overcome barriers and motivate yourself to find work.*
- ✓ *Different techniques to apply for jobs.*
- ✓ *Why your covering letter and CV are so important and how to improve them.*
- ✓ *How to understand what employers are looking for.*
- ✓ *Different types of interview and how to perform better at them and win.*
- ✓ *Five key questions you must be able to answer.*
- ✓ *What to do if you are offered a job and how to keep it.*

✓ *Lessons to learn from not being offered a job and how to improve.*

✓ *How you could use your passion to create a business niche for yourself.*

Getting a job is more difficult now than before but not impossible. If you can make some changes in your attitude, outlook and action you will get back into work.

If that's what you want, then continue. It may not be easy and you will have to commit yourself to wanting to get back into work. It will be a fusion of your desire, commitment and ability to change that will lead you down the road to employment.

Don't expect that by just reading this book you will succeed. I'm just giving you the tools. You have to take them and use them if you want to get yourself working. If that sounds like you, then read on.

CHAPTER ONE

The Myth About There Being No Jobs

As a trainer of the unemployed I'm always surprised at being told there are no jobs out there. One look at how many recruitment sites there are online and the thousands of jobs on offer tells a very different story. Think about the economy you live in and how many people are working.

In the 1980's in the UK there were about 3 million people unemployed out of a working population of approximately 30 million. Today official figures suggest there are under 2 million people out of work in Britain but there is an overall population of approximately 65 million people living here. Latest figures show there are 13 million children, around 11 million people retired and 6 million students. That means there are well over 30 million people doing something to earn money. Does that sound like there are no jobs?

In the world now there are jobs, but the rules of engagement have changed. Employers know there are more candidates looking for work. They are being pickier about who they employ. They put in more hoops to jump through to get the job. They want to pay less and expect a lot more from employees.

There are also more part-time positions and there is a growing need for greater flexibility as well as contract and short-term positions to fill a pressing need.

It doesn't matter what field you are in (except ones where there is a limited supply of talent and those with them can demand high wages, like professional footballers), what you can earn now is less than you might have received a few years ago.

With that in mind you need to prepare yourself for a very different jobs market from the one you may have been used to. Gone are the days of expecting an employer to pay over the odds to keep you on or to spend money when it's not required. Many firms now just hire people when they're needed.

If you've worked in a certain field for some time, you may have got used to a good salary and benefits package. The problem comes if you are made redundant or lose your job and have the same salary expectations. The whole industry might have moved on since you did the job and you will likely either need to upskill, retrain or take a lower wage.

For many of you this will seem hard to swallow but it is the reality in which we now live. To become employed will take a complete change of thinking in order for you to succeed at getting a job. You may need to do more than one job in order to make up one full-time position.

However, before you start tearing off and applying for every position under the sun, take some time to think about yourself and the skills you have to help you find work. You should also consider exactly what you want to do. That is your starting point.

CHAPTER TWO

Seven Steps to Find What You Want and Plan How to Get It

When most people talk about work they have no set plan about what they do or why they're doing it. You might just have slipped into a career or job because it came along and you could make money to pay the bills. If your situation changes and another job doesn't come along, you may find yourself unemployed.

The longer this goes on the more desperate you feel about it and the harder it is to motivate yourself to find work. This is when you need to think carefully about where you are and what you want to do. Instead of just applying for anything, think about what you **REALLY** want to do. This is a perfect opportunity to re-evaluate what you want from work and life, and plan your way forward.

The Big Plan

Think carefully about what you want to do. Is there a job or position you think you could do? Do you have the necessary skills for it? If not, can you get them? Look at the industry you are targeting. Can you find out where the opportunities are? Do they pay what you expect or are you going to have to take a wage cut?

You are essentially targeting a specific market. You are now not randomly applying for any job. You now have a clear focus on what you want to do and can move towards it. By planning, you are eliminating a lot of wasted effort, energy and heartache.

It is very much like a journey from A to B.

A   **FOCUS**   **B**

Diagram 1

'A' is unemployed and 'B' is employed. To get to 'B', you have to know where you're going and have a plan to get there. Knowing what you want and being clear about it will help you achieve it. Having a focus is an important element in finding work. You might look at it as a journey.

For example (see diagram 2, opposite), in the UK if you decided to go from London (A) to Edinburgh in Scotland (B), you wouldn't just get up and go. You would plan how to get there and which route to take. Along the way there could be problems; a roadblock, accident etc. You have a choice; sit in it or find another way.

A   **FOCUS**   **B**

Diagram 2

In the employment market it's the same. If you apply for jobs in a certain field there may be barriers to entry. People will find reasons not to employ you such as age, or a lack of qualifications or experience. If you're serious about working in a certain industry you are going to have to find a way through this.

As with everything much depends on your desire to get a job. Nothing is easy. What are you prepared to do to find employment? The key here is to find a way through or take an alternative route to get to your goal.

Know Yourself Better

Most people don't really know themselves that well. They think they do but they don't. If I asked you how much time do you spend working on yourself, what would you say? How can you develop yourself further? What do you need to do to get the job you want? These are questions you should ask yourself and then take ACTION.

I would suggest that one way of finding out about you is to do a SWOT analysis. What are your STRENGTHS and

WEAKNESSES, where are the OPPORTUNITIES and what are the THREATS (or what's stopping you achieving your goals?). Be honest and write down exactly what you are all about in each category.

By doing this you have a much clearer understanding of yourself. It also gives you the opportunity to analyse yourself and to make changes where they are needed. It's important you realise this as part of understanding something about yourself. Remember you are going to have to sell yourself to employers and knowing about yourself in a lot of detail will make it easier to do.

Using this technique and writing down information about the most important person in the whole process (namely you), you have a much better chance of seeing what you have to do to achieve success. You should be brutally honest with yourself and know what you have to do to move your life forward.

If you find this hard, ask others (family and friends) to help you. Ask them to be totally honest. Take their critique not as criticism but as FEEDBACK. Use this to implement the changes you need to find work.

Listen to Yourself

Too many people never listen to themselves. At times your mind is telling you what to do but you never take it up and just let it pass. For example, how often when you sit quietly on your own do you get random thoughts running through your head?

Simplistically this is the creative side of your brain talking to you. It is the voice of the inner you speaking to you. A good way to listen to this is to make time for yourself every day to find what your inner you is saying. Capture these thoughts and write them down in a diary. Go back to them in a few days, discard the bad ones and act on the good ideas.

A lot of this is your intuition. Internally you know what you want but carry on doing what you've always done because it's easy to just do that and get by. If you harness the power you have within you and find what you really want to do, start moving towards it.

The saying "you have all the resources you need within you" is so true. Sometimes the voice in your head is telling you what you should be doing but often you ignore or let it go without taking action. This method may help you find what you're really looking to do with your working life.

Get out of the "I Can Only Do That" Syndrome

There is often the feeling that if you have done one thing all your life you can't do anything else. Another feeling is you can only do it one particular way. All too often you are in the comfort zone and don't like getting out of it. It's easy to fall into this trap as so many of us do or have done (including me). You see, we do things in life for two reasons; either to get pleasure or to avoid pain. Sometimes these are bad habits that have been learnt.

Doing work we don't like is hard as it goes against this, but needs to be done because it pays the bills.

The truth is we are all learning machines and learn new things every day. You can also unlearn things that you don't need or use. This may be disturbing and cause problems, but in life sometimes you have to do things you don't like to achieve what you really want.

Something else you can do is change your habits. Do things differently; nobody is hardwired to do things in one way. You can change. Some changes are more difficult than others. If you can't or don't want to make a massive change, go for something smaller.

Even if it's small differences, over time you can build on these and together they can make a major difference. The aim is simple – to move you towards new thinking and fresh ideas about you and your future. It's not just in terms of your employment prospects but also in all areas of your life.

Make Decisions and Take Control of Your Life

A lot of people put being unemployed down to being the victim of circumstance. There's always a reason they are not in work. Everything is outside their control and they can't do anything about it. That could be you. Can you hear yourself talking about why you can't get a job? How others are luckier than you?

Take a step back for a moment and ask yourself, "If in my life I had taken a different path, would I be where

I am now?" The answer is probably no. We are all the makers of our own destiny. The choices you made in the past have determined your position now. So how do you get out of it? How do you break free from it?

The answer, my friend, is to make some new decisions. You can't rewrite the past but you can change the present and create a better future. It will mean thinking differently about yourself. If you've followed what I said before you should be well on the path to new thinking about yourself and where you want to be. The power to change rests with you. Choices you make now can shape your future destiny. So make some key decisions about where you are now and where you'd like to be.

Change Your Language Patterns

If you're unemployed or looking for work you tend to think negatively; "I can't do this," "I can't do that". You are talking yourself into a feeling of negativity. Everything is difficult. The whole vibe is one of there is nothing you can do and you are the helpless victim.

One thing you can do if you feel like this is to change your thinking. Refocus your mind. Change from "I can't" to "I can". Begin to tell yourself you are able to find work, that there are jobs out there and you are going to get one. Tell this to yourself constantly. It's amazing how quickly you can start thinking and acting differently about your prospects of finding a job.

Before you start saying this is just that same old positive thinking stuff that never works, think about it carefully. Whatever you feel comes from the way you think. Your thoughts are the cornerstone of how you feel about everything and you can change them in an instant. If I told you you'd just won a million pounds on the lottery, would that change your feelings? They'd switch in a heartbeat.

By shifting your language patterns and internal dialogue you can change the way you feel about almost anything. It is an important tool you should learn to use and get the best from in all areas of your life especially if you're looking for work.

Mindset plays an important part in how you approach your search for employment. You have to believe that you will get a job and that can only come by thinking differently about it and refocusing your mind.

Reinvent Yourself

Another way you can bring about change is to reinvent yourself. Change the way you look, dress and feel. If you are serious about work then act as if you want to get a job. Look the part each day. Be professional in your outlook. Dress to impress not just others, but yourself. You want to be seen as someone who is ready to work and really wants it.

A new look goes hand in hand with new thinking. Even if you are short of money you can find ways to improve the way you present yourself. It's amazing how others will see you; "projection is perception". What you put out is what others will see in you. Changing your look will help you develop both personally and professionally. Others will react differently to you and it will change your own, and others' perception of you.

Taken Together

When you put all these things together you can see the essence of what you can do to transform yourself and your life. Reinvention is nothing new; look at those who have done it all their careers. Madonna and David Bowie spring to mind. They have continually changed themselves and attracted a growing audience for their work. Employability today is the same. You have to change yourself to fit today's market if you want to progress. If you fail to change you will be left behind. Today's hi-tech world is moving extremely fast and you have to keep up if you are to progress.

You now have seven points to address to get yourself back into work. If you're looking for your first job or the first one in a long time, then this process is crucial for you to succeed.

EXERCISE 1

1. *Take time to think about what you actually want to do. Have a plan in mind and start moving towards it. Write down what it is you want to do and think how you can achieve it. Speak to those doing the job you want and find out how they got it. Copy or use them as a blueprint to achieve your goal of getting a job.*

2. *Know yourself better by writing down your personal qualities. Write down ten things about yourself that tell everybody all about you. You can't use the words honest, trustworthy, reliable, hardworking or punctual. (I'll mention this again later when we discuss CVs).*

3. *Listen to yourself. What is your inner self telling you? Take time to listen to yourself and the thoughts you come up with. What are you telling yourself that you should be doing? Write down your thoughts and refer back to them after a few days and take action on the good ones. This will help you understand yourself much better and move you in the right direction.*

4. *While you're finding out about yourself stop thinking you can only do one thing. Consider the skills you have and how you can use them to get work. What else can you do? Can you transfer these to other sectors? Could you sell your skills to employers in another field? Write down what you have done and how this could be transferred into other sectors in order to get you back into work.*

5. *Make decisions about what you want to do and then take the appropriate action. Without doing this you are drifting. You need to be clear in your mind about what you want. By doing this you have focus and clarity. Both are important in finding work. Together they will help you take control and move your life in the right direction.*

6. *Change your language patterns. Go from saying; "I can't" or "there isn't" to "there is" and "I can". Much of what you tell yourself will manifest in your life. It's not just about being positive, but also telling yourself that you can succeed. Self-talk is part of the process of reinforcing in your mind what you can achieve. By repeating it constantly you will get there. As they say, "repetition is the master of skill".*

7. *Revamp the way you look and how you are seen. Reinvent yourself and show how different you can be. Remember this can only help you change the way you are perceived by others. If you are seen differently you may get a positive response.*

   What you put out in the way you look or sound or act can help you get into employment.

These are some of the personal development methods you can use to get back into work. Much of this is to do with change and how you deal with the world around you.

CHAPTER THREE

Barriers, Motivation and Changing Your Story:

How to Break the Habits of a Lifetime and Get Working

If you've completed the exercises from the last chapter you should now be a lot clearer about what you want to do. The more focused you are, the more chance you have of finding work. It's like throwing a dart; if you have no board or anything to aim at, how can you score? Football with no goals wouldn't be much of a game. Now you see why it's important to focus your mind on what you want and start moving towards it. The clearer you are about what you really want, the more chance you have of achieving it.

You also need to raise your level of **MOTIVATION**. How much do you want to work? What is the driving force behind your striving to get a job? In reality most people say they want to work but are not as motivated as they could be. They're half-hearted, maybe because they're supported by a benefits system or they simply just don't want it enough. So how do you raise your motivation level? What can you do to change it?

Consider motivation to be a bit like a thermostat. If you want to turn it up you have to have a reason. So using a heat analogy, you will need to raise the temperature if you are cold; the colder you are, the more you turn it up and the hotter you will get.

In terms of work, think about how much you really want something. Think about your own life and a time when you really wanted something. It might have been a car, a house or a fancy outfit. In your mind you had to have it no matter what. You might have even become a bit obsessed about it. Now you have to apply the same thinking to getting a job.

Think about how you are going to achieve what you want. Do you have the skills, the qualifications and experience to be successful? What steps can you take to get there? Who can help you achieve your work goals? Now you're in a much better place to start formulating a plan of action to become employed.

If you really want to do something, as opposed to doing it just for money, you are much more **ENTHUSIASTIC** about it. If it is your **PASSION** – something that's your hobby or something you **LOVE** – you will be much more motivated to do it. That is something you should consider. Maybe you could turn a hobby or interest into a business.

If you really want to raise your motivation level then my advice is do something you love. Part of the reason I'm writing this book is I'm passionate about helping people achieve personal success. As a trainer, I love to engage with people and positively affect their lives. This is an extension of that process for me.

So what else is stopping you getting a job? What comes next is crucial to your success.

Overcoming Barriers

All too often you fail to achieve what you want because you are put off by failure or the thought of failure. How many have times have you been told that you can't achieve something for whatever reason? It's a recurrent theme in life that even those close to you use. Something isn't possible because people like you don't do that kind of work, only a few can achieve success, or you're not good enough to do that. You give up or find an easier option and get by without achieving your dream or goal.

How many of your dreams have been scuppered by that type of thinking? How often in your life have you stopped doing something because others said you couldn't do it? Life is full of examples like this because others think you can't do it so you don't. You're paralysed by the doubts of others and never try to achieve what you want.

Before becoming a trainer I worked in radio and television news as a presenter, producer, reporter and programme editor. After completing my diploma in radio journalism my course tutors said to me, "You're a nice guy Oni, but we don't think you'll make it in this industry".

For me, the biggest motivator is being told I can't do something. I am always on a **MISSION** to prove people wrong. For two years after that I travelled the length and breadth of the UK working in 22 different radio stations taking whatever shift came up until I achieved my goal of working on LBC Radio in London on the AM Breakfast Show. That was my dream as a student; to work on a programme I listened to every day. The rest, as they say, is history.

If you are serious about working, you have to have an almost **OBSESSIVE** desire to get what you want. Using my travel analogy from before and diagram 3, consider it to be a journey from A to B.

Diagram 3

You're going along but then there may be obstacles and barriers put in your path. There's no train, the road is blocked or there's a traffic jam. When this happens you have a choice. To stay where you are and accept it or to find another way around it, over it or under it. It's here that **PERSISTENCE** and **DETERMINATION** come into play. Your reaction to these setbacks will determine your eventual outcome.

How much you want it and your desire to get there are in many ways more important than qualifications, your background or what you've done in the past. There will always be barriers to entry into any industry no matter what you do. If you are serious about achieving something then you have to give it your best shot and go for it. Don't get deflected by others or be put off by naysayers. You have to want it more than other people and be almost **OBSESSIVE** about achieving it.

Here are some typical barriers and ways to overcome them.

1. Age

   I am sure that despite legislation and laws about not discriminating on grounds of age such discrimination still exists. Nevertheless, I also feel if you are determined to do something then you can achieve it so long as it is REALISTIC. I wouldn't for example say you could become a professional singer or brain surgeon without a high degree of skill and, in the latter case, being highly qualified as well.

If there is something you really want to do you should strive to do it no matter what as long as you have the skills. Age is only an issue if you allow it to be. If you are serious about doing something, then get in front of people who can help you achieve that goal. Research and find out from those doing what you want to do how they got there. You need to find out as much information as possible about the role you want and whether there are opportunities to pursue it.

Don't let age stand in your way. It is, after all, just a number. You need to believe that whatever your age, you have wisdom and experience that is invaluable and that you are highly employable. If you get in front of an employer, you will need to convince them you are the right person for the job whatever your age.

2. Lack of Experience

Be realistic about your prospects. If you're told there are no opportunities or they go to those with more experience, try to get some. See if you can volunteer and get some first-hand knowledge and work experience of what you want to do. You may also spot opportunities for yourself in that sector or elsewhere. If you find a niche and get yourself in, build on it to improve your chances of either becoming indispensable to the employer or to move into whatever you want to do. If you do voluntary work don't consider it to be free; everything you do has a value. Yes you are giving your time, but it is gaining you valuable

*information, experience and a reference for
other employers.*

*You need to be able to build on what you have
to make yourself more marketable to potential
employers. The more you can show you are working
to move yourself in the direction of a chosen career
path, the more you become a credible candidate in
that field. Finding ways of getting experience is a
key tool in getting back into work.*

*Get in front of those who can help you achieve
your goal. Don't ask them for a job, ask them for
an opportunity. Go and talk to them about what
you want to do and convince them to give you
a chance. Use this to build your knowledge and
experience in your chosen sector and get
yourself working.*

3. Lack of Qualifications

*Lack of qualifications for jobs is always an issue
these days. Employers are now using them as
hurdles, which you need to overcome to qualify for
an interview. Yet history has shown people with no
qualifications being successful and more successful
than those with them.*

*If what you choose to do requires you to be
qualified, then you need to see if you can get the
relevant qualifications. Another way is to convince
an employer to take you on and pay for you to
be trained. This is what happened in my case. For
over 20 years I was a radio and television news
producer but left the profession in 2009. I studied
to be a life and business coach as well as becoming
a master practitioner in NLP (Neuro-Linguistic*

Programming), which I did myself as part of my journey into teaching and training.

In 2010 I was offered the chance to train the long-term unemployed. To do the job you need a teaching qualification called PTTLS (Preparing to Teach in the Lifelong Sector). My first employer who gave me the training opportunity paid for me to do it on their time. In my second position I was told I needed an IAG (Information Advice and Guidance) qualification. This was again paid for by my employer while doing the job. Along with my teaching and training experience this now gives me much more credibility when applying for positions within the industry.

Lack of qualifications should not stop you pursuing a particular career path. While employers today expect you to have them or be prepared to gain them, not being qualified doesn't mean you can't succeed. Many employers will pay for training as it's in their interest to have properly qualified staff. If you have issues over cost speak to your boss and convince them to help you get them as I did. Ultimately your success in whatever sector will be determined by your persistence and your ability to get whatever is required to succeed in your chosen field.

4. Self-Talk, Mental Games and Other Barriers

A great deal about getting into work now is down to your mental attitude. Most barriers start in people's heads. First there is the notion there are no jobs. I think I've dispelled that myth and the myths that your age, experience and qualifications won't get you the job you want. I've told you the steps that can be taken to overcome these barriers.

In the next chapter I'll discuss the importance of getting your message about wanting work out to the world. By repeating this message to other people you are also telling yourself you want work. I also spoke about changing focus where you start to believe there are jobs and you can get them. This is reaffirming it to yourself in your own mind. You are now thinking about the possibilities of work; that's a very different mindset from that with which you started.

Where you are now has as much to do with your internal dialogue as everything else. If you've been telling yourself there are no jobs, that becomes the situation for you. To overcome this you must change your story; tell yourself you will find work and there are jobs out there.

You should now start to believe more in yourself and start to anticipate opportunities. That doesn't mean you sit back and expect it to happen like the law of attraction. You should be making a determined and consistent effort to make things occur. There is no substitute for digging for what you want and putting yourself out there.

In general, if you tend to believe you are where you are because of circumstances that are out of your control, that's simply not true. You are where you are in life because of decisions and choices made in the past. If you had made different decisions and choices you would be in a different place. So, if you want change, make different choices.

If you are going in one direction with life and it is not working, you can change direction. Break free from what you are doing and where you are now by simply making a different decision. Challenge yourself to do something different. You don't have to make big changes, small ones will do. Each small change will have a cumulative effect on your life. By running a different strategy you will get a different outcome.

Success in whatever field you want comes through a combination of action coupled with desire and determination. Nothing comes easy. It takes effort to achieve what you want. You need more than blind faith in the world and you need to put into effect a combination of changes that will help you achieve your desired goal.

Getting a job or finding work is no different. When there are fewer jobs than before, you need to do things differently if you are to succeed. Below are some steps you can take to start that ball rolling.

EXERCISE 2

Motivation

Think about your level of motivation towards finding a job. What level is it at on a scale of 1 to 10? If it's below 10 how can you raise it? What do you feel will drive you to want a job more? Remember it's like a thermostat; you need to turn it up if you want to succeed. Write down your motivating reasons for finding work. Keep these near you and constantly remind yourself of why they are so important.

Age

If you are older (like me, over 56) don't assume you are on the scrapheap and are unemployable. Consider where you are and what skills you have to offer any potential employer. Think of all the work or jobs you've done and the skills and experience you have that could help their business. How could you add value to the company? What do you bring that others can't? How can your skills fit in within the firm? This is particularly important if you want to change professions.

Qualifications

If you are trying to enter a particular field, find out which qualifications are needed to do the job. Do you have what is required? Can you get the required qualifications? If you do, will an employer take you on? If not, can you volunteer and get some experience? Talk to those in the industry you want to enter; ask them about potential jobs in that sector. Find out if you can target specific jobs.

Overall qualifications are just an entry ticket to jobs. It's how you perform and come across to employers that's important. And remember, sometimes they will pay to train you if they think you will fit in their organisation.

Self-Talk

Think about what you are telling yourself about work and your internal dialogue. Is it negative?

If so, can you change it? Can you refocus your mind and start telling yourself there are jobs and opportunities out there? Keep repeating this to yourself and talk to others about what you want. This is part of the inner dialogue you must change in order to think yourself to success.

Mind Games

Everything starts with a thought. If you can think about what you want and know you have the skills to achieve it, then the chances are you can achieve. Believe you can find work and start working towards it. Remember you have to put in the effort to make it happen. Write down what you have to do. Put it on a post-it and place it where you can see it every day as a reminder. Make a plan of action and move to make it happen. Your action will say more about you than any CV you send out randomly.

Belief

Write down what you believe about yourself now. Think about where you are now and where you want to be. What do you now feel about the future and your chances of success? What can you now do differently that would have an impact on your life? Write these things down and make a plan to implement them. If you take action you will see that things begin to change and you will move in a different direction.

Summary

Take these steps and you will start to understand yourself a lot better. This is part of the process that will help you shift your thinking and move you closer to finding a job.

The truth is you have all the resources you need to be successful. You just need to recognise them and harness their power to achieve success in all areas of your life.

In the next chapter I'll be talking about how to search for work and what you need to do to make the most of opportunities that arise.

Summary

CHAPTER FOUR

Where to Look for Work and Make Opportunities Happen

Having taken time to find out about yourself and make some changes in what you want to do, you now need to think about how to find and apply for jobs. This time though it won't be random or a scattergun approach but a *FOCUSED* and *TARGETED* one. You will be clear about what you want and have some idea of what you want to do.

With jobs harder to come by it is important you use a range of different strategies to find work. You can't just rely on one method as doing so can seriously limit your success. The most common error people make is just applying for jobs they see advertised either online or in a newspaper, yet this accounts for just a fraction of the jobs market. Only 20% of jobs are advertised; 80% are taken before that. You see employers, like most people, are short of time and want quick solutions. This is the

HIDDEN jobs market and is something you need to tap into to find work.

Many bosses will ask their employees if they know anybody who can fill positions. If they can find someone without having to advertise, they can save themselves a lot of time, effort and money.

From your perspective it is the best way of finding work. If you are recommended by someone, then the chances are you will have little or no competition for the post. The fact that someone who is employed by the company puts you forward means that you are already half way to getting the job. It's worth remembering that when you are recommended by an employee, they have an established relationship with the employer who trusts their judgment. So a lot of the work has been done before you even get an interview for the position. These are usually the best type of jobs to get.

So here is the first thing to do to get into work using this method:

1. Speak to people you know or don't know

   Being unemployed shouldn't be a stigma these days. There are periods when everybody may find themselves without a job. It's happened to me on a few occasions, so I'm not speaking as someone who has never been there. I've always found that talking to people who are working can be a highly effective way to find work.

Talk to everybody you can to see if they can help identify potential opportunities. Talk to friends, family, old colleagues, even someone at the bus stop. You will use this method to get yourself out there. You need to be talking or networking with anybody and everybody who can help you get that elusive job.

Using the word-of-mouth method has a dual impact particularly in terms of language patterns and what you are telling yourself. Firstly it gets the message out that you are looking for work and it reaffirms your commitment to yourself to find work.

Nothing is better for the soul than reminding yourself that you are actively seeking work and that you are out there getting that across to others. Always be prepared to put yourself forward and be ready to sell yourself to potential employers. Continuous networking is a vital tool in finding employment.

If you hear of jobs through a third party, contact the company and offer your services. Make sure you have an excellent covering letter and CV telling employers exactly what you have to offer them. Being proactive is important in helping you get back to work.

2. Using the Internet

The most effective way of applying for jobs is the internet. The problem is that most people using this method fail with their applications. Their CVs, though received, never get a reply or end up somewhere I call "CV cyberspace"; a kind of black hole for redundant CVs nobody ever sees. Remember, in a recession employers are looking for specific skills and can pick and choose who they hire. The internet allows employers to filter out people they don't want unless the CV hits the right mark. Think of the process as being like a giant funnel and filter (see diagram 4). An employer gets 1000 CVs and then cuts them down and interviews ten, second interviews four, and employs one. Online applications are really a way of finding reasons you shouldn't be employed.

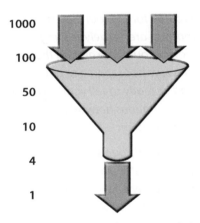

1000

100

50

10

4

1

Diagram 4

From your perspective you may wonder why after sending off a CV (sometimes without a covering letter) you never get a reply. Is there a reason for it? Is there a way to get seen or get an interview? It all depends on the CV you send and if you tick all the right boxes and have the right KEYWORDS. What are those, how do you find them and why are they so important?

Because of the large numbers of people applying for jobs, employers are increasingly SCANNING applications. The scanner is looking for keywords. These are usually in the JOB ADVERT and JOB SPECIFICATION. You will need to read these carefully before you apply for a job. I'll talk more about this in the next chapter.

Ensure your covering letter, CV or application form contains those key words so that you will have a better chance of securing an interview. Without them your chances are slim. This is nothing to do with you but it is the way candidates are selected for interview. The system is looking for reasons to exclude people from the process and pick who are considered suitable candidates.

3. Newspapers and Magazines

Newspapers, both national and local, advertise jobs. Application can be online or via letter. Whichever method you use, make sure you always send a covering letter. This is vital as it tells the employer why you are writing to them.

You can also use the newspaper stories as a source of information, for example, when a new factory or other business is opening near to you. Be proactive and offer your services early. Be clear about the skills you have and how they could help their organisation. Always remember you are selling yourself to potential employers and have to put across what you believe they are looking for.

4. Local Area and Beyond

Wherever you live, always be on the lookout for new developments, shops or offices and potential new companies moving into your area. Approach them either with a CV and covering letter or ring them directly. Again, your aim is to sell yourself to them, so consider what they might be looking for and how you would fit into their organisation.

Don't just look locally; look at areas a little further away. It's like fishing. If there are no fish in the pond or river you're fishing in then try a different pond where you might have better luck. Too many people limit their searches to a small area. Broadening the search will open up more opportunities. That's exactly the kind of thinking that's needed to get working.

If you're prepared to move further afield you might find even more jobs available. Much is dependent on how much you want to work, what you will do to get a job and where you would go to work.

5. Broadcast Your CV

If you look online you will find hundreds of recruitment sites offering thousands of jobs in different sectors. Apart from applying for jobs you can also post or broadcast your CV. You simply upload it to the site and you can be found. This is a good way of getting in front of potential employers who are looking to recruit staff. Using this method I have personally been approached and gained work from employers looking to hire people.

An important thing to remember if using this method is to regularly update your CV. That could just involve changing a word or sentence and refreshing it on a regular basis.

The reason for this is that once you put the CV on, it starts to move down the pile. Imagine other people putting their CV on top of yours so yours is pushed down. Refreshing it regularly (say once a week) keeps your CV near the top of the pile. Visibility and being near the top of the pile are very important when recruiters are looking for candidates.

6. Social Media

In today's world social media has become an important tool in finding work. One way is to join a professional network like LinkedIn. This is particularly useful if you are in a specific profession. You can find other professionals who you can connect with and target when looking for work. This is a highly useful tool for getting jobs.

Another method you could use to look for work is Facebook. This is an alternative way of connecting with people you are friends with and you can ask if anybody knows of potential jobs. They might have friends who are able to help you find work.

On top of this you could use Twitter. Tweet the kind of work you are looking for amongst your followers or those you follow and see if it brings any results.

7. Offer Yourself for Free

I'm quite taken by a method shown on the website **www.businessballs.com** *in a section called "How to Get a Job in Tough Times". This comes from the website and is not my own idea. Elsewhere in this book I will show you how to tweak it to get good results. Essentially the site suggests you put together a flyer where you offer to work for free for a period of time to prove yourself to employers. This is taken to different local companies in person and you engage with staff to ensure the message gets to the managing director or boss of the company.*

It's claimed, "this no-nonsense approach changes the way you will feel about being unemployed". The aim is to shift your mindset. It says, "you effectively make getting a job your full-time occupation and you don't give up until you get one".

I can't argue with the method or the idea behind it. The aim is to keep going until you achieve success. According to the site, "many people won't want to try it as it calls for a high degree of confidence and motivation to undertake it". It adds, "if you do use it you will find many people supporting and commending you on your desire which is good for your soul and self esteem". For the full method go to **http://www.businessballs.com/jobhunting-method.htm**

8. Shops, Newsagents, Phone Directories and Other Sources

I thought I'd just mention these as they might prove a good source for job leads. Always be on the lookout for potential jobs. Occasionally you find shops advertising jobs or a local newsagent with a card in the window.

Follow up potential leads. These kinds of adverts usually put you in direct contact with employers so you need to be prepared to be interviewed over the phone (more on that later) or in person (remember, first impressions count).

You could also use phone directories or local Chamber of Commerce and business directories to target specific companies. You could write a speculative letter asking for work, but I think there might be a better way.

Why not contact the company and ask to have a chat about potential opportunities? The aim is to get in front of the boss or the person hiring staff. Get talking and build rapport. Even if they don't have a job they might know others who do.

9. Be Proactive and Be Different

Whatever you do, make sure you are proactive in your approach to finding work. Be clear in what you want and put your mind to achieving your job goal. As they say, "where the focus goes, the energy flows".

You could also try doing something different. There have been examples of people standing on roundabouts or by motorways who have put themselves in front of a different audience and have been successful at getting a job. The aim is to do the unexpected and get noticed.

If you're serious about getting work, do more, be more, achieve more. Make getting employment your mission. If you put more into getting work you will get more out of the process and hopefully find yourself a good job.

For me, nothing beats meeting people and pressing the flesh. Meet as many people as you can and tell them all you are looking for work. If you remember what I said before, there is only one aim and that is to get yourself working.

Much of your success will be dependent upon how you can sell yourself to potential employers. People buy into people. If an employer buys into you as a person, then there is a good chance of getting a job. I'll talk more about that later as I believe too many people think they should be employed because they have the right qualifications. In my opinion people get hired because they are not only qualified but also because they are LIKEABLE and can FIT into an organisation. That is the key to understanding why people get employed.

Summary

So there you have some different steps you can take to get yourself employed. Getting into a job requires you to apply a range of different methods if you are to succeed and not just rely on the internet and newspapers.

In the next chapter I'll focus on applying for jobs using covering letters, CVs and application forms and the rules to follow to be successful and secure an interview.

CHAPTER FIVE

Applying for Jobs:

Rules for Covering Letters, CVs and Application Forms

By now you should have planned the kind of work you want to do, looked at different ways of finding work, got over your barriers and re-motivated yourself. You now need to start applying for positions.

The most common way to apply for jobs is online. It's quick and usually easy, but there are rules you should follow that will help you succeed in getting over the first hurdle and securing an interview.

Always remember when you put in an application for a post you are in competition with others. In order for you to succeed you have to have what the employer wants and then be able to convince them you can do the job. Any person in business is short of time and needs to see you are the right candidate quickly. That means whatever you send has to stand out, and if your application is scanned it needs to have the right keywords and tick the right boxes. (See previous chapter about scanning.)

You should also bear in mind that with hundreds or even thousands applying for the job, potential employers are looking to exclude candidates from the process. The more you can do and offer a company and if they feel you could add value, the more chance you have of getting an interview.

So here's what you should be doing if you want to have your application considered.

Application Forms

I'm starting with application forms as a lot of what you'll need to do here will be essential for covering letters and CVs. The way in which you now have to fill in such forms is the basis for applying for jobs in general and has some important rules you should follow.

The first thing to understand is that an application form is different from a CV. It can be much more specific about what the employer wants to know. They may ask your age (not required on UK CVs) or qualification grades (can be left off CVs) or even specific information about what you have done in the past and your suitability for the position.

Before you start filling in any application form make sure you **READ IT** through thoroughly. You need to know exactly what information is required and in what form you should put it. The biggest mistake you can make is simply tearing off and filling it in without going through it first.

Also, before you start you should read the **JOB SPECIFICATION** very carefully. Check that you have the right qualifications, skills and experience required. You should also look at three different areas that are crucial to your application.

These are:

ESSENTIAL SKILLS: What are the essential skills you must have to apply for this job? These could include job specific qualifications, certain types of experience, skills vital for the role. If you don't have them there is little chance of your securing an interview unless you know or have been told to apply even if you don't meet the requirements. Otherwise you shouldn't apply; it's not really worth it.

DESIRABLE SKILLS: These are not essential to the application but are a bonus if you've got them. In essence, if you come with additional skills and training it's an extra the employer might be able to use. It may also enhance your chance of getting an interview over other candidates.

HIDDEN SKILLS: You also need to read between the lines to see what might be required to do the job but is not explicitly stated. So if it were a security position you might need tact and diplomacy as well as the ability to undertake conflict resolution. Overall you are going to have to look at the position and consider what might be needed and expected by the employer in the role.

After you have done this, check the **KEY WORDS** or phrases that are in the job specification and job advert that you will need to use in your application (usually in the additional information or personal statement section of the form). This may be crucial in the selection process for interviewees.

The reason for this is that these days with so many applications they are **SCANNED** by machine rather than read by a human. They are looking for keywords in applications and to filter out those that don't have them. That is why it's so essential to have them in the completed form and they could be the difference between getting an interview or not.

Filling in Forms

If you are filling in an application by hand, copy it first and get your wording right and layout presentable in rough before you complete it for real. It's also important that you fill in application forms in **BLOCK CAPITALS** and in **BLACK INK.** The reasons for this are twofold. It ensures the reader can understand what is written and if it is copied or scanned it is legible.

There is another reason that goes hand in hand with what you should do next. Make sure all the boxes are

FILLED IN, especially the ones not relevant to you. Put a line through them or put in **N/A** (not applicable) or **N/K** (not known). This is important for the scanning process.

Scanners are not human and can only work under their own conditions. In the case of using black ink, some scanners don't recognise blue ink. As for empty boxes, the scanner assumes the form is incomplete. In both cases applications are rejected on those grounds. It is simply the way scanners operate and it's important you understand that.

The starting point on all application forms is your personal and contact details including phone numbers and email address. After this it will probably be work history. Put in your most recent position, when you worked there and what you did. On application forms they can ask you to be more specific. They can ask you the month or exact dates so there is no hiding. You can also be asked why you left. Overall, however you apply, employers are really interested in what you've done in the past ten years. The only reason you might want to highlight other areas is if they're relevant to the position.

Once that section is complete you should do the same with your education and training history. Put in your most recent qualifications first and work backwards, including where and when you studied and the qualification you achieved. Some forms also ask you to specify the grades you received (which is not good if you got poor grades).

Additional Information

This is probably the most important part of the form and so it requires the most thought. You need to put in details about why you should be considered for the position. Make sure you put in the key words or phrases from the job advert and job specification. Tailor your skills and experience to show you are a credible candidate. The main thing to understand is that this is the chance for you to really sell yourself to employers and you should take the opportunity to do just that.

Competency Based Answers

Some application forms will ask you to answer specific questions about what you have done and how that relates to the position. In these cases you might be asked to give specific examples of what you did and the eventual outcome. For example, they might ask how you dealt with an issue involving conflict resolution, team work or anything that the employer might be looking for.

The best way to answer these questions is to use the **STAR** method. **SITUATION:** What was the situation you had to deal with? **TASK:** The task you had to undertake. **ACTION:** The action that you took. **RESULT:** What was the final outcome?

If you are looking to change career or move into a different field this might be relevant as you will have to tailor your answers to show how what you've done in the past can be transferred into another sector.

Overall the employer is looking for a specific range of skills and the answers you give will determine if you are invited for interview. The more you can show you have what they want, whatever your background, the better the chance you have of being selected for interview.

Online Applications

Online applications are now more commonplace than ever. You fill in an application online rather than filling in a specific form or supplying your CV. There are issues and perils you should know about and be prepared for when using this method to apply for jobs.

When applying online make sure you have all the key information to hand so you can put it straight into the form.

Some sites will allow you to do the application in stages but all too often they are **TIMED**. You can only apply within a certain amount of time when filling in online forms. I have often had clients working on an application and they take a break or look for information to put in and they come back to find their application has disappeared and they have to start all over again.

The rule here is to be **PREPARED** for an online application and not get caught out.

Covering Letter

It is said that **FIRST IMPRESSIONS** count and this applies to written applications. You have just a few seconds to convince employers they should look at your CV. That makes the covering letter the most important **MARKETING TOOL** you have. It is the first contact you have with employers and it has to impress them. In essence it has to sell you to them and give them a reason to look at your CV and consider you further.

In my time in the employability sector I'm amazed at how many people apply for jobs and don't include a covering letter. Admittedly, sometimes that isn't possible, but in general you should include one if you can. The reason why it's so important is that it introduces you to potential employers and lets them know why you're writing to them. Without one they could be confused about what you want or what you're applying for especially if they have more than one position to fill.

As with the application form and CV your covering letter should contain some of the keywords you've found in the job specification. It should be structured in three parts that follow a logical process that I feel works well.

If you are sending your application online then make sure you put in the job you are applying for and any reference details in the subject line so there's no doubt why you are writing.

I have read that you should send the covering letter as an attachment. Personally I wouldn't do that. In an age when people, including employers, are impatient, waiting for an attachment to open could be time consuming and if it takes too long your application may be deleted. I'd put it straight into the body of the email so the recipient knows why you're writing and can read your covering letter immediately.

On the next page is a typical covering letter you would send out to potential employers:

34 West Street
Tellingham
East Essex
TT7 8NT
TEL: 07767 870945
Email: rsmith676@tnmail.com
23 Sept 15

Mr J Ford
Employability Limited
23 The Street
London
EN5 7UP

Dear Mr Ford

I am applying for the position of Employability Trainer with your organisation as advertised on the Givemeajobnow.com website.

For the past three years I've worked for a wide variety of organisations delivering employability and a range of related courses to help people get back into work. These include customer service, facilities management, CSCS (Construction Site Certification Scheme), retail works and hospitality.

I have worked with a wide range of individuals from different walks of life including single parents, young people and ex-offenders. All of them had different issues that I have helped to resolve.

To help me achieve my goals I use life and business coaching skills as well as NLP (Neuro Linguistic Programming) in which I am trained. Fused together these give me a powerful range of tools to help people shift their mindset and get back into work. As well as this I have a formal teaching qualification PTTLS level 4 and IAG (Information Advice and Guidance) level 3 which I have gained while in the industry.

Within this field I have been highly successful and contributed to the success of every company I have worked with and I believe I could do the same for your organisation.

Thank you for considering my application and please find attached my CV, which highlights my career to date. I am available for interview at any time and look forward to hearing from you soon.

Yours sincerely (for a named person)
Yours faithfully (for Dear Sir/Madam)

Richard Smith

You start your covering letter with your contact details in the right hand corner. Leave a line and put in the date. Underneath this on the left hand side you put in who it is going to. It is better if you can find the name of someone to send it to, or you can put in "to whom it may concern" and then company details.

Underneath you put Dear Sir/Madam or a named person, so in this case Mr Ford.

The first part of your letter tells the employer why you are writing to them, what you are applying for and where you saw the advertisement. A point to note here is that if you were told about the job by someone who works there then mention them. This will give you brownie points as the employer can immediately associate with that person as a reference as there is already a working relationship.

The second section of the letter is all about **YOU YOU YOU!** Sell yourself to the employer telling them about your work experience, skills and qualifications. You can use this section to add any recent information that might not be in your CV such as training and qualifications you have achieved or are studying for and other work experience such as volunteering. This is really the best opportunity to tell the employer why you are the best person for the job and why they should look at your CV and give you an interview.

The third part of the letter wraps things up. Always thank people for considering your application (good manners never hurt!) and tell them your CV is attached along with your availability for interview.

To end, if you are writing to a named person it is "Yours sincerely" and if it is to Dear Sir/Madam it is "Yours faithfully". After this leave 4–5 lines and type your name.

The cover letter is really your opening gambit and an introduction to employers. As I've mentioned before, it is about the impression you create with employers and should be well laid out, error free and convey your suitability for the position.

To ensure this make sure you print a copy off and check it yourself and ask others to check if it has mistakes and if it explains why you are the right candidate. Make sure you use one of four different fonts. Be aware that modern computers naturally default to Calibri but older versions of Microsoft Word don't recognise it. This is important as all versions of Microsoft Word recognise these fonts.

So use either:

- ✓ **Times New Roman** (the normal default, but it's hard on the eye)
- ✓ **Arial**
- ✓ **Verdana**
- ✓ **Tahoma**

You should also use the covering letter to make speculative enquiries about jobs. As always, timing is important and if your CV and covering letter arrive when a new job arises or someone leaves, then you may be in with a chance of getting an interview.

One way you could try and get in front of employers is to ask to come and talk about possible opportunities. You could use this to gain valuable information about the company and how it works as well as selling yourself to the employer.

Speculative Letters

It is important to realise when you're looking for work that the vast majority of jobs are never advertised. As I mentioned earlier, eighty percent of jobs are filled without the company looking or advertising for staff. So when you see any position online or in a paper it's only 20 per cent of what's really out there. The "hidden" jobs are usually filled by employers asking their staff if they know anybody who is suitable for the position. That's why it's always good to network with people who are working so they can alert you to potential jobs and give you the name of the person to contact. This is a very good way to find work.

Alternatively you might try writing to companies with a speculative letter to see if they have any jobs. You never know, your letter may arrive on the boss's desk just as someone is leaving.

The format for the letter is the same as the covering letter except on the first line you would put something like:

Dear Sir/Madam or named person (Mr Smith/Mr Jones),

"I am writing to see if you have any vacancies within your organisation".

If someone who works at the company has told you about a job, then mention them by name. It's important you do this as if they're employed or known to that person they have an established relationship and trust their judgment. This may mean your application is fast tracked to the interview pile or the competition is narrowed down to none as no one else is considered.

So the covering letter, be it in response to a job advert, responding to something you've been told or a speculative offering, is an important way of introducing and selling yourself to a prospective employer.

That leads me on to the second marketing tool to get back into work, the CV.

Curriculum Vitae

The CV is probably the second most important document you will have to get in front of an employer. It is quite simply a rundown of what you are all about, what you have done in your career, your work history, education and training, and anything else that might be relevant to getting a job.

Having sold yourself with your covering letter, the CV has to be even more impressive to convince the employer to invite you to an interview. He or she has to feel after reading it that you can do the job and are worthy of being seen.

Below is a standard structure CV that I would suggest you use. There is no right or wrong way to write a CV; the only aim is to make sure it works, and if it doesn't you need to change it.

NAME ADDRESS

CONTACT DETAILS

INCLUDE PHONE NUMBER AND EMAIL

PERSONAL PROFILE

KEY SKILLS

EMPLOYMENT HISTORY

Year   Company   Position

EDUCATION AND TRAINING

Year   College/School/University   Qualifications

ADDITIONAL INFORMATION/HOBBIES
AND INTERESTS

REFERENCES AVAILABLE ON REQUEST

Now let's look at this standard layout in detail.

NAME

ADDRESS

CONTACT DETAILS

PHONE NUMBER AND MOBILE

EMAIL: T.MALONE@UONLINE.COM

This is how and where an employer can contact you. You should include home, mobile and email details. You can put them left, right or in the centre. The choice is yours. I always put it in bold to **HIGHLIGHT** it and **MAKE IT STAND OUT.**

You don't need to put "Curriculum Vitae", at the top as it is obvious what it is. In the UK you don't have to put down your date of birth, nationality, marital status, sexuality, religion or political beliefs and you don't need a picture of yourself.

The next part is the MOST IMPORTANT section.

Personal Profile

Again, it's all about **YOU YOU YOU!**

It is your chance to sell yourself to employers. This part of the CV has to tell them just how good you are and what you've done or the qualities you have to make you the right candidate.

Avoid the following words at all costs. **NEVER** use them for job applications.

- ✓ *Honest*
- ✓ *Hardworking*
- ✓ *Trustworthy*
- ✓ *Reliable*
- ✓ *Punctual*

They appear so often in CVs they have become totally meaningless. If you are applying for a job you should remove all of the above. Try to use more powerful words such as dynamic, forward thinking or highly motivated. You should keep it short, punchy and to the point, highlighting your best qualities. If you have done more, you can extend it by putting in important information about what you've done or achieved in your working life.

There are a few rules you should be aware of when compiling a CV. These go back to what I mentioned in the application form section.

Remember to read the job advert and job specification looking for the **ESSENTIAL, DESIRABLE, and HIDDEN** skills that are required. Make sure these are put into your CV as well as the **KEY WORDS** that are also included. This may mean you have to write a **DIFFERENT CV** for every job you apply for, tailoring it to meet what the employer is looking for.

Remember employers are short of time and they want to find out all about you in this half of the page. This will be the first thing the employer will look at after the covering letter. It has to convey to them what you have done and why they should invite you to interview.

This makes the next part very important.

Key Skills

- ✓ *Keep them short and punchy (on one line if possible)*
- ✓ *They should show what you are REALLY GOOD AT*
- ✓ *No more than five key skills*

✓ *Use bullet points to make them stand out*
✓ *Any more than five will look like a row of dots*

This is followed by:

Employment History

DATE: EMPLOYER   **POSITION**

Employment dates
Who you have worked for   The position you held

Start from your most recent position and work backwards. Employers are really only interested in the last 6–10 years. Underneath the above you need to talk about the kind of work you did and your role in the job. Some people use bullet points, but I prefer about 5–6 lines about what you've done.

For the CV you can leave out months. This can hide a multitude of sins, especially periods of unemployment.

Education and Training

DATE: SCHOOL/COLLEGE   **QUALIFICATIONS**

When you were there
Where you studied   Your qualifications

Go from your most recent qualifications backwards, adding dates, the place or name of where you studied and what you obtained. You don't need to put your grades in (unless they're brilliant!) as they are irrelevant unless you are just out of school, college or university and this is your first real job. It's another reason for employers to exclude you from the interview process.

Hobbies and Interests/Additional Information

What do you do in your spare time? Mention hobbies or interests that may show some other skills not on your CV. For example, do you run a darts team or volunteer somewhere? Are you active in your church or local community? Add anything that shows other skills you may have that can be used in a job.

One woman I trained with was a single mother who had not worked for five years. When I asked her what else she did in her spare time she told me she had managed events for her church for five years. This wasn't even on her CV but might have helped show what she could do in a job. This section also gives an insight into what you are all about. Always remember that employers are people and they are in the business of hiring people they can work and connect with. If you share a common ground or interest with those taking on staff it may work in your favour.

Refer back to some of the ten things I asked you to write about in the first chapter, telling me everything about yourself. These can be added in here or in the personal profile. Your aim is to underline areas of your life that are a reflection of you beyond what you do at work and these can paint a fuller picture of you as a person.

Diagram 5

Like completing a jigsaw puzzle, employers are looking for people who are a certain shape and the right size for their organisation. They also want staff who join them to fit in and share commonality with them. This makes hobbies and interests an important part of the process.

References

Current thinking is that you put "Available on Request". Personally, I've always mentioned my referees by name. Once it worked in my favour as the employer knew the referee and spoke to him before the interview, which led to me getting the job.

Make sure you speak to your referees and know how to contact them. They should be aware you have nominated them so when they get a request for a reference they are prepared.

If you can't find your references because companies have moved or closed down, what can you do? Google your former employers by name. If they work in a certain industry you might be able to track them down. Using this technique I helped one client who had been trying for a year to find a previous employer. We found him online and this helped obtain the reference he needed which led to a new job. References are a key part of securing employment and knowing where referees are and getting them to respond to new employers is key.

> ****NOTE**** Make sure you print off both your covering letter and CV and read them through **THOROUGHLY** to spot mistakes. Often when looking on screen you miss things that can be spotted on paper such as missing full stops and punctuation or spelling errors. Never leave this to chance. Your CV and covering letter should be error free. It doesn't look good if you say, "I pay attention to detail", but have glaring errors on your application.

Another tip is to ask other people to read it. Make sure they understand what you have written and ask them if they received it would they offer you an interview or a job. Sometimes it takes others telling you to change things that will make you do it rather than keep sending out a CV that isn't working.

Summary

Overall a CV should be no longer than two sides of A4. I've mentioned the four fonts you can use (Times New Roman, Arial, Verdana and Tahoma); also make sure you use a large enough font size (12) as anything smaller can be very difficult to read.

When it comes to making a choice about candidates, employers are people and they are buying into people like themselves. They are investing in you as a person and have to like you as an individual and see you as part of their organisation. Sometimes they will forego qualifications if they feel you are the right candidate for their company. It's about whether you will fit in and are the right shape for them to mould or move into the role and whether you can be developed to add value to their company.

Diagram 6

The CV is a sales and marketing tool for you. Treat it as one and it will serve you well. If you are applying for a range of jobs in differing sectors you might need to have different CVs for each one. This may also be the case when applying for all jobs where you tweak your CV to include the keywords and skills that are in each job specification.

While this all might seem annoying, it is the reality of the working world today. Getting a job is harder, but by understanding how the process works and what you need to do, there is no reason to be unemployed. You need to apply new thinking in order to achieve success.

Now you know what you need to do, here's a checklist of actions you need to take now to improve the way you apply for jobs.

EXERCISE 3

1. ***Practise filling in an application form.*** *Use a black pen and block capitals. Make sure you put in all your personal details and any information required by the employer. Then add in your work history followed by education and training using the method above and starting with the most recent first and working backwards in both cases. The additional information is the most important part and should be tailored to show what you've done and why you are the right person for the job.*

   Make sure every section is filled in, even the ones not related to you (do not fill in boxes that say for "office use only" as they are for the employer). In those you don't fill in you should put a line through or the words N/A (not applicable) or N/K (not known). Also ensure you have signed and dated it.

2. ***Rewrite your covering letter.*** *Follow the method earlier in the chapter and structure it into three parts. The first should be your introduction explaining why you are writing to the company.*

Remember you can apply for jobs or send out speculative letters to see if companies have any vacancies or if you've been told of potential positions by people you know or through contacts you've made.

The second part of the letter should be about YOU YOU YOU! It concerns what you've done and why you are the right person for the job. Remember to add any qualifications and training you might be undertaking or work you are doing, for example volunteering, or maybe something relevant to the job you're applying for.

The final section should thank the employer for considering your application. Give details about your CV and what you would like to happen next. Always end on a positive note, possibly reiterating your desire to work for the company.

3. **Rework your CV.** *Rewrite your CV using the method above. Start with contact details and then continue with profile (again talking about yourself). Unless you are a graduate or applying for your first job your work experience is next. Employers are really only interested in the past 6–10 years. However, it is important to include all recent employment history with no gaps (unless you can explain why you weren't working). Go from most recent to the first in reverse order.*

Education and training are next. Again, the same rules apply starting with most recent first and then going backwards. Additional information and hobbies and interests come next. This shows employers what you do in your spare time and could highlight other skills that may be useful in the job.

Finally, if references are requested, look for people who you have worked with or who can vouch for you as a person. They might be people in your community or those that know you well. They cannot be family, relatives or friends.

For all these sections make sure you have run off a hard copy to check for mistakes and errors and get someone to read it to make sure it makes sense.

NOTE With these three sections it is important you have access to them especially when you are out. Two ways of doing this are to have the information in cloud storage or on a portable USB stick to access on a computer. I would also suggest you email them to yourself. That way if you're out and spot a job you could go to a library or internet cafe and access them. This could speed up your job-hunting opportunities. The digital age has made it possible to store and access information electronically and that should be used to ensure you don't miss applying for jobs as soon as you see them.

CHAPTER SIX

Get Yourself Noticed by Employers:

Direct Methods of Applying for Jobs

Phone Companies

One of the easiest and most direct methods of trying to find work is to ring up companies directly. You can look up numbers in local phone directories or online and compile a list of organisations you are targeting to apply for jobs.

If you do phone them, ask to speak to someone who deals with hiring people in the company. Try to avoid their HR departments, as they tend to work to bosses' orders about taking on staff. It might be better if you've done some research and found out the name of somebody in authority you can contact and speak to directly.

When phoning there are rules you should follow, and I will go into more detail in the next chapter when I talk about telephone interviews. In general, though, make sure you are in a quiet place where you won't be disturbed. Be prepared for it and have your CV handy in case you get asked questions, along with a pen and paper to write things down.

Speak slowly and clearly and listen carefully before answering questions. If you get asked to send in your CV make sure you get the name of the person to send it to as well as the address/email address and send it off as soon as possible.

You could have a script ready to use and make sure you practise what you say. Rehearsal and repetition is the key to success (more on this in interview techniques in the next chapter).

Go Directly into Businesses

Another great way of trying to find work is to go directly into businesses and ask them if they have any vacancies. If you do so you can use the method I mentioned before and suggested by **www.businessballs.com*** (How to Get a Job in Tough Times) and **http://www. businessballs.com/jobhunting-method.htm***. I must stress the technique is not mine but I've tweaked it a little to what I feel would improve it.

According to the site "this method says a lot about you as an individual and your desire to find work. It also puts you in charge of your destiny and should give you a sense of empowerment". The method suggests "you are appropriately dressed and get into rapport and engage with people you meet in order to get them to help you find work. The level of engagement is key to your success". For the full method go to **http://www. businessballs.com/jobhunting-method.htm**

It goes on to say "even if they don't have anything at the moment make a note of where you've been and go back to them in a few months' time". If you think of direct marketing, junk mail or emails, you are continually sent material whether you want it or not. A lot of the time you bin it, but every once in a while something takes your eye and stands out and you decide to buy. They've been mailing you for months or even years to see if you can be encouraged to buy.

You have to take the same approach with your desire to find work. Get yourself and your CV in front of people regularly. Try different approaches and be persistent in whatever you do. Luck doesn't just happen; you have to give it some encouragement. That requires you to persevere if you want to be successful.

So here is what you can do to get in front of employers and sell yourself to them. Being persistent is a key to successful job hunting and securing work.

EXERCISE 4

PHONE COMPANIES: Make a list of organisations you could call about work. See if you can find out who to speak to. Practise what you are going to say to introduce yourself and ask about job opportunities. Remember first impressions count so how you speak is very important. Be prepared to get a lot of "nos". Don't take it to heart but move on to the next call. I believe this direct approach can bring rewards if done properly.

GO INTO LOCAL BUSINESSES: Again, make a list of local companies you can visit in person. Go suitably dressed and take in either your CV or the flyer you can make from Business Balls (**http://www.businessballs.com/jobhunting-method.htm**)* *offering your services free for a week. The method says that you can distribute 30–50 flyers a day. I would work with fewer, simply because you can target specific businesses you would work for and this will help you focus on getting a job you want and will keep.*

If you do as I've suggested before and know the type of work you want to do, then target those specific businesses. Maybe target ten a day; that's fifty a week and 200 a month. I'd also write, memorise and practise a guide script that you can use. As I've said before, practice is the master of skill and the more you do it the better you will become. Engaging with strangers is not easy for some people and the only way to improve is to repeat it regularly.

In the following chapter I'll be looking at the next and crucial stage of the job-hunting process, namely the interview. For most people it is a daunting prospect, but it needn't be. With some help, preparation and practice you can succeed and find a job.

*©http://www.businessballs.com/jobhunting-method.htm

CHAPTER SEVEN

Interview Techniques and What Employers Want

If at this point you have made changes to yourself, your outlook, motivation and desire, your application forms, covering letters and CV, you should be seeing some results. I've found that people start to receive replies (some more quickly than they expect), and in some cases it's led to an interview and job offers.

That is the aim of this whole exercise. Just reading the above will do nothing unless you take action. That means shifting from what you've been doing to trying something new. In the field of employability there is no right or wrong. Everybody thinks what they do is right. In truth, it's only right if it works and gets you into work. If it doesn't it is wrong and you need to change it again until you succeed.

I see so many people who say they're sending out multiple CVs and getting no replies. The obvious answer is what they're doing isn't working. It is effectively broken. If it were a car or a bicycle that wasn't working properly, you would get it fixed. It's the same with applying for jobs; if the methods you use are not working, fix or change them.

Having effected changes in applying for jobs you now need to work on your interview techniques and understand what potential employers want from employees. In a recessionary period it's vital you understand what they are thinking to ensure you can convince them you are the right candidate for the job.

What Employers Want

With the economic readjustment continuing, it seems more and more people are applying for positions, particularly low-skilled jobs. Working for UK supermarkets is now much tougher. Part-time positions are now highly sought after. In fact, many people are applying for jobs that they are overqualified for because it's the only work there is available (or so they think).

From the employer's point of view it means they can pay less and demand more. They are more selective about whom they employ and they keep raising the bar for qualifications and skills they now want for jobs that in the past didn't require them. With a ready pool of labour they can pick and choose who they want.

More than ever they are looking for an individual who is the right fit for their organisation. They want someone who is the right shape and who can be moulded into the role. The more value you can add to the role the better. If you think back to the job specification for positions for which you're applying, remember the essential, desirable and hidden skills and qualities employers are looking for. The more you meet them, the better your chance of securing an interview and getting the job.

So let's look at what you should do if you are offered an interview. The first thing to say is well done! All your previous hard work has paid off.

Now you've reached this stage there is action you need to take which is vital to get a job today as you may be in competition with many other credible candidates.

If you are lucky enough to secure an interview then your covering letter/CV/application form have worked. The employer has seen them, read them and thinks you can do the job. Now all you have to do is convince them that you are the right person.

Research

When you are offered an interview it's important to do some research about the company. The employer usually asks you what you know about the organisation as part of the interview. The boss will want to know what you think about them and what you have found out prior to the interview.

You could look at its size, structure, and which markets it is in. You should know about it from the point of view of its organisation and have an idea about the job you are going for. Most of this can be done online. If you want to find out first hand you could ask to visit the company before the interview. Overall you should be able to answer at least one question about what you know or have learnt about the company.

There is nothing worse than being asked about an organisation you want to work for and knowing nothing about it. It is crucial you research and prepare for such a question and have an answer around 30–50 seconds long.

Prepare Questions to Ask

Have questions ready about the job and the role. Think about the position you are applying for and what you'd want to know about. At the first stage avoid questions about pay, holidays and pensions (they can come later).

You could discuss their expansion plans, how the job role will grow and chances for promotion and training opportunities. I would say ask between 3–5 questions related to the role and the company.

Prepare your Interview Answers

It's always difficult to know what you will be asked at interview but you can be sure they will be looking to find out more about you and for evidence that you have done what you have claimed. After my time in the employability sector I can think of five key questions you must be able to answer to succeed at interview. They are:

✓ *Tell me about yourself*

✓ *What do you know about our company/ organisation?*

✓ *What are your strengths?*

✓ *What are your weaknesses?*

✓ *Give me a reason to employ you. What sets you apart from other candidates?*

If you can successfully answer these five questions you have a good chance of getting a job. Let's run through these one at a time and explain what's required.

1. Tell me about yourself

The employer wants to know about what you have done in your working life, starting with the most recent job and explaining the role you had and the duties you performed. Make sure you emphasise the successes you had and how the role developed. Work backwards through your other jobs again, explaining what you did and how that relates to the position you are applying for now. Also add in any new information about training or qualifications you have gained while working.

Employers are really interested in what you've done in the past 6–10 years; anything before that is not that important unless you are looking to return to a field or profession you've done in the past. If that's the case you need to emphasise this more than your recent work.

2. What do you know about our company/organisation?

This is where your research comes in. You have to be able to talk about what you know about your prospective employer. Most of the information you can find out from the internet. This could include the company's structure, mission statement, values, their chief executive and the markets they work in. You don't need to know everything about the organisation, but enough to give a good solid answer of around 30–50 seconds. Overall this shows not only your interest in the company but also that you have some knowledge and understanding of how it operates.

3. What are your strengths?

You need to be able to sell what you are really good at to an employer. You may have listed these in your key skills. If you say you have a particular strength be able to back it up with evidence. That means using real examples of what you have done. A good way to answer these types of question is using the S.T.A.R Method (see the last chapter regarding competency based answers on application forms). That is – start with the SITUATION you were confronted with and the TASK you had to undertake, then mention the ACTION you took and the RESULT or outcome. This will give the employer a good idea of how you deal with specific problems and issues in the workplace. Make sure you emphasise your role in this and what you did to ensure the final result or outcome.

4. What are your weaknesses?

This is always a difficult one that people often don't have an answer to. The truth is you MUST be able to answer this question as it says a lot about how much you understand yourself. It doesn't mean you have to show where you are vulnerable or weak but that you know there are areas in your life where you could do better.

I would take something you are not good at and talk about what you are doing to resolve the issue or get better at it. It can be something simple such as administration or overloading yourself with work. Don't use things that could put you in a bad light such as getting to work on time or getting out of bed. The aim is to show you know where your weaknesses are, that you can improve and that you are doing something about it.

5. Give me a reason to employ you. What sets you apart from other candidates?

Probably the most important question you will be asked. This is your chance to shine in front of a potential employer and tell them why you are the right candidate for the job. It's here you need to be memorable. Think about all the qualities you have (and don't use honest, hardworking, trustworthy, punctual or reliable). Think of what you have that makes you different from the competition. In business they call it a USP (Unique Selling Point). This will differentiate you from the rest of the market and show the unique qualities you have.

If you go back to the exercise in chapter one where I asked you to write down ten things that tell me everything about you and you use some of those, you will definitely stand out from the crowd. When I talk about being memorable it's because the moment you walk out you don't want them to FORGET YOU. When they are reviewing candidates at the end of the interview process they have to have a reference point to remember you by and the answer you gave. That's why the question is so important.

NOTEThere is a current vogue for slipping in questions that make you have to think on your feet. Here are a few examples that have been used:

1. *If you were a colour, what would you be and why?*

2. *If you were an animal, what would you be and why?*

3. *If you were a Disney character, who would you be and why? (One of my students was asked this. His reply was, "Mickey Mouse, because he's been around the longest").*

In an interview employers can ask you anything they want. It's important you are **PREPARED** and **READY** for whatever you will be asked and that you have answers. You should think of this as being like a rolodex of information you are going to sift through at speed and give the right answers.

Review

At this stage I would stop and think about the answers you would give at an interview to the above questions. You need to be clear about how you would answer the questions. You could write out the answers in full, although I would just make notes on what you'd say and how you would say it. Sometimes if you learn what you've written down it sounds stiff or fake and that's what you want to avoid.

> ****NOTE**** A key thing to remember is that as well as preparing your answers you need to **PRACTISE** them. The problem with interviews is that we don't do them often and in the end it is down to your **PERFORMANCE**. Consider this. If you were the leading actor in a West End or Broadway show you wouldn't just turn up on the opening night and give the performance of a lifetime. Before the public performance, you would have rehearsed it time and time again. You would have worked out what went wrong and how you could improve in order to get it right on the night.
>
> They say that practice is the master of skill. The more practice you have, the more chance you have of spotting mistakes and errors you make. If you can iron them out at this stage there's less chance you will make them at the real event.
>
> If you want to perform better at interview make sure you have **REHEARSED** it not only to yourself but to other people. See if they like your answers and refine them if they don't. By tweaking them you will be able to give a better performance and hopefully get the job you want.

Preparation Before the Interview

Plan your route

Make sure you know how to get to the interview. Plan the route you will take to get there and if necessary do a trial run. Know an alternative route to get there just in case there are traffic or transport problems. Have contact details to warn employers if you are running late.

Arrive on time

On the day of the interview make sure you arrive in good time (about 15 minutes before). You will need the time to cool down/warm up, go to the toilet or get into the right headspace. Many people are nervous before an interview (which is totally understandable) and you might need the time to calm down before you go in. What you should remember is that you should not consider it as an ordeal. If you've been invited to an interview the employer thinks you can do the job and are close to getting it. All you need to do is convince them you are the right person. Don't fear interviews; embrace them as being a step closer to getting employed.

Look the part

Dress appropriately for the job. In general that means a suit for men and jacket, skirt/trousers and smart top for women. The aim is to look professional and create the right **IMPRESSION.** First impressions count and you have a very short while to achieve this – about three seconds. Someone will make a judgment decision about you the moment you walk in the door.

In terms of dress, you should tailor it to the job you are going for. If it's construction or factory work then smart casual is probably acceptable. For ladies it is best not to wear too much makeup or stiletto heels. Again this depends on where you are applying to. If it's a beauty parlour or a shop specialising in high-end shoes (Jimmy Choo or Christian Louboutin) then those rules go out of the window. It comes down to what is appropriate for the job and that is a judgment you have to make yourself. If you've had the chance to visit the company before the interview see how people working there are dressed and dress appropriately.

Also make sure tattoos are covered up (unless the job is in a tattoo parlour, or somewhere known to be very accepting). They may be fashionable but are viewed differently by many employers. Some have now banned them and won't employ people with them. So be aware of the impression tattoos can make and the impact it can have on your obtaining employment. Make sure what you wear is clean and ironed and not crumpled up. Again, this is to do with the impression you create with potential employers.

Hygiene

It is important you not just look but also smell the part. I am amazed at how many people forget about this. You should bathe/shower before an interview, and brush your teeth. Try not to eat spicy or heavily seasoned food beforehand as smells can linger. If you are going to wear aftershave/perfume don't make it too overpowering, as you might be in a confined space at the interview.

Smoking and drinking

If you are a smoker, do not to smoke before the interview. Employers will be able to smell it. Also avoid drinking alcohol either on the day or the night before; this could impact on your performance and also give the employer a bad impression.

The interview starts here

The interview process begins the moment you walk into a company. You are being judged by the people you come into contact with, so be aware of the receptionist or anyone else you meet in the organisation. How you come across to them might have a bearing on your employment prospects.

Different Types of Interviews

One-to-one interviews

These are the standard ones involving you and the employer. It is just the two of you in a room. When you are met by the interviewer, shake their hand firmly and look them in the eye. When invited to sit down do so, ensuring your feet are shoulder width apart and flat on the ground. Place your hands on your knees so you can use them to gesture as you speak. Try to sit a little forward and relax your shoulders. By doing this you are creating a solid foundation and a position of strength from which to speak. Don't move around on the chair or fidget as this is distracting. Make and keep good eye contact and have good body language. This is important. Body language makes up more than 55% of communication.

In the past interviews were usually one-to-one or to a panel. While this still holds true, employers are using other types of interview as part of the selection process. You should be aware of these so that if you have to take part in them you are well prepared and ready for them.

Panel or more than one interviewer

Sometimes you might have more than one interviewer, which can be daunting. If you are in such a situation it is important you get and stay in rapport with the interviewers. Use the seating position as above and keep good eye contact. You do this by looking between the eyes of the interviewer asking the question and holding it for about ten seconds and then moving along to the next person and doing the same to everyone on the panel before returning to the first person. This takes a little practice but should help you engage better with those interviewing you.

I'll return to both of these later in the chapter where I will spell out in more detail what to do and how to perform better at interview.

For the interview you may also take in a few copies of your CV to hand out to panel members who might not have seen it. Also have any documentation, certificates, qualifications etc. and in the UK your passport or birth certificate, and your right to work and reside in the UK along with National Insurance number.

Phone interviews

These have become increasingly commonplace in recent times and are easy and quick for employers to undertake, so it's important that an employer has your contact details and can get hold of you at short notice. Make sure your phone numbers (mobile and landline) are on your CV and covering letter so you can be contacted.

A phone interview fulfils a number of different functions. Firstly, it shows if you can **COMMUNICATE** with the employer (an important skill to have). Secondly, it is a chance for them to gauge if what you wrote on your CV matches what you say.

It can also be used as a **COMPETENCY** based interview to find out if you have the skills they are looking for. It is a **FILTERING PROCESS** to exclude those who don't match up to what the employer wants.

There is an assumption phone interviews are less formal than face-to-face interviews; I can assure you they are not. They are an integral part of the job selection process. Be aware this method is very common these days and it is vital you understand what to do if you are contacted.

If you are called up to be interviewed over the phone make sure that it is convenient. You don't want to be on a bus or out and about. If you are called and you are not in a suitable place, ask if you can do it later or ring them back when it's convenient; that way you can prepare before the interview.

When you do finally undertake the phone interview here are some tips and suggestions to help you succeed.

1. Landline *not* mobile

    If possible undertake any phone interviews on a landline rather than a mobile. That's because you can guarantee the signal and there is less chance of being misunderstood or the line becoming crackly or going down. If it's not possible then make sure the place you are doing the interview from has good signal strength.

2. Go to a quiet place

It's important you go somewhere where you won't be disturbed or distracted. Make sure it is quiet and you are ready and prepared to answer questions you will be asked. Ensure pets, children and relatives are out of the way for the duration of the interview.

3. Have information to hand

Have a copy of your CV or the application form you sent in to hand so you can refer to it when you are asked questions. You can also scan through the job specification and be aware of the kind of person/ skills they are looking for when you answer.

4. Stand, **don't** sit

When you are being interviewed stand up rather than sit down. When you stand up you speak very differently. By doing this you change the dynamics and speak with more authority. Stand up straight, legs shoulder width apart and stiffen your body. This will create a kind of chi board. This is a power position and you will speak from a point of strength when being interviewed.

5. Smile when you answer

When you answer questions put a smile on your face. When you do this it changes your tone (which is a really important part of communication) and this will make you sound better. It will soften the way you come across and your answers will have a more positive impact. It's worth practising smiling to use this at interview.

6. Listen and answer slowly

Listen to the questions and answer slowly. If you don't understand what's being asked, repeat the question back (this will buy you some thinking time). Otherwise, ask for the question to be asked in a different way.

7. Be polite and speak nicely

Always remember you are being judged by someone at the other end of the phone. Make sure you don't swear or curse, and answer questions in a friendly tone and manner. Likeability plays a big factor in deciding whether you get interviewed.

8. CBI (Competency based interviews)

Sometimes telephone interviews will be competency based. The employer is looking to find if you have specific skills to deal with different situations that they feel can occur in the job. You will need to give specific answers to the question being asked. I've referred to the S.T.A.R method before where you take the Situation you are trying to resolve and the Task you had to undertake. You will need to explain the Action you took, your role in it and the eventual outcome or Result at the end. Your answers could be scored on a scale of 1–10. The nearer you are to 10, the more chance you have of being employed or selected for a final interview.

9. Thanks and what next

Always thank the interviewer for the opportunity to speak to them and ask what happens next in the process. You essentially want to know what the next move will be on their part and when you will hear about the next stage of the interview process.

10. Feedback

Before you conclude the interview make sure you can get feedback on your performance even if you don't go any further. This is CRITICAL. If you made mistakes it's important you know about it and can rectify them for future interviews. You can only improve your performance next time if you know where you went wrong. You can start ironing out the issues now so you don't make the same mistakes again in the future.

Summary

As with everything connected with interviews, **PREPARATION AND PRACTICE** are the keys to success. The more prepared you are for what will happen and the more practice you get, the better you will perform. Remember to practise doing interviews on the phone. They say the secret to success is repetition and the more you repeat something the better you will get at it. It's the same with live interviews. Practising is a warm up for the real thing. So when you come to do interviews make sure you've taken the appropriate steps to succeed.

This leads us on to:

Group Interviews

These too are becoming increasingly commonplace especially if there are a lot of candidates looking for work. Supermarkets and retail outlets use them a lot. They are looking for certain qualities such as teamwork and the ability to get ideas across in a group situation. They might also be looking for leadership qualities. Being in a group situation means that you have to **STAND OUT** from others. You will have to interact and show you have the qualities they are looking for.

Always remember that while you are in this type of situation you are being observed. People are grading and marking your every move. You could be asked to take part in a problem solving exercise or sales tasks to see how you work with others. Each exercise will be designed to test particular skills.

I know of one major supermarket that has a 17 page document it uses to score candidates. This shows you how companies select their staff, and that's just for a sales assistant's position. Another American retail company uses the group interview to get interviewees to sing songs and interact with each other. Obviously they are looking for a level of performance from their sales staff.

There may also be a short interview as part of the process so you will need answers to the five key questions mentioned earlier in this chapter. Alternatively they might have a quiz or exercises to undertake. Only those who've made a **POSITIVE IMPRESSION** will go forward to the next stage. That might be a more formal interview.

Assessment Days

These are similar to group interviews and can take up a whole day. The exercises can be similar to those in the group interview and how you interact with others will be observed. The interviewers might also be looking for candidates who stand out and those who have leadership qualities.

As part of these days there will be a number of exercises and scenarios to deal with. Each will be looking for specific skills the employer believes are important for the job. Another element might be **PSYCHOMETRIC TESTS,** which are sometimes used for graduate or higher-level positions. These are exercises looking at different skills.

I'll run through four of them.

- ✓ *Numerical*
- ✓ *Verbal*
- ✓ *Diagramatic reasoning*
- ✓ *Situational judgment*

The last one is also growing in popularity as an initial screening for graduates.

Numerical reasoning

These tests look at how candidates deal with numbers and their accuracy and speed. The tests have questions that assess your knowledge of percentages, ratios and rates along with cost and sales analysis and currency conversions.

Verbal reasoning

The aim here is to get candidates to read short passages of writing and then answer questions that assess comprehension of the text. The tests are really to assess the ability to think constructively rather than looking at vocabulary or word fluency.

Diagramatic reasoning

These are designed to assess logical reasoning ability. To do this, questions measure the ability to infer rules shown on a sequence of diagrams or a flowchart. The aim is then to see how the candidate applies the rules to a new situation.

Situational judgment

Using these tests candidates need to show how to approach situations in the workplace and the candidates' suitability for specific job roles is tested. Amongst the aspects being looked for are communication and influence, teamwork, relationship building and customer focus.

In addition to these there are other areas that can occur including personality questionnaires, aptitude and critical thinking tests and inductive reasoning. In essence they are looking at how you approach and deal with different situations using your mental abilities and thinking skills.

I don't want to go into too much detail as there is a wealth of information on the internet about them, as well as tests you can buy, or do for free. If you are going to do them for real you should do some practice tests so you get a feel for what kind of answers you will have to give to be successful at passing them.

One-to-one/Two/Panel Interviews (revisited)

These remain the ones that most people have either as a first or second interview for jobs. To win at these everything mentioned at the beginning of the chapter is relevant. It's worth reviewing all the points to ensure you are prepared; arrive on time, look the part and make sure you have practised the answers you will give to questions you may be asked.

If you have been invited to an interview they must think you can do the job. It's now up to you to convince them you are the right candidate. Try not to be nervous; it's not a grilling. Try to be yourself and be calm and collected.

When you enter the room shake hands firmly with the employer and make good eye contact with them. A firm handshake, smile and looking them in the eye should demonstrate your confidence and also make you seem trustworthy. I personally hate limp handshakes, because it always makes me think I can't trust that person.

Making the right **FIRST IMPRESSION** is vital. You only have about three seconds to achieve this so looking the part is key to success. If you don't, there's little chance of your getting the job, even if you're the best-qualified candidate. It's how you're perceived by the interviewer that's the most important thing.

Remember the employer is looking for someone who is the right fit for their organisation. The employer has to make a judgment about you as a person from the moment you walk through the door. Will you fit into the organisation? Do you look the part? Can they see you being involved in their company? Do they see you as part of their team? And will you add value to the organisation?

Wait to be invited to sit down. When you do sit, don't slump back in the chair. Also try not to cross your legs. Put your feet shoulder width apart flat on the floor and sit a bit forward and straighten your back. Like standing, you want to create a power position where you have authority and can answer effectively and confidently. You should place your hands on your knees and use them to gesture when you speak. Try it out for yourself.

It might be a bit uncomfortable as you have got into bad habits in the way you sit and stand. This brings us neatly on to.

Body language

The way you hold your body is very important. In communication it is the most important factor. It is said body language (how you hold your body) is about 55% of communication. I think it's much higher. Here's an example. If you are attracted to someone, you know straight away. There's no, "well, I half like someone", because you know exactly what you like. There are no half measures. I'd say body language is about 85% of communication, but let's stick with our original figures.

The next most important aspect is the **TONE** of your voice. That's about 38%. Body language and tone therefore make up the bulk of your communication. Most of it is in non-verbal form. So, speaking in the right tone is crucial in how you are perceived by potential employers. As they say, "it's not what you say, it's the way you say it" that's important.

The **WORDS** you say make up just 7% of communication. So if I refer you back to when you're attracted to someone, if you are sold on them and they're sold on you, what you say makes little difference. It's the same in an interview. If the interviewer and you like each other's body language and you have a **RAPPORT** with each other, there's a good chance you'll get the job. Added together body language, tone of voice and a few choice words can help you become successful at interview.

However, before you run away with the idea that body language is the most important factor you also have to realise that an interview is also about your **PERFORMANCE** on the day and once you are in the interview room you have to be totally **PREPARED** to ensure you win.

Putting together body language, tone of voice, performance and being prepared is the key to being successful at interviews.

The show starts here

You're now in front of the employer and should be fully prepared for what comes next. You should have done your research on the company and be ready to answer questions about yourself and what you've done in your working life. This is really about selling yourself to the employer.

As you are in the correct sitting position you are ready to begin. Refer back to the start of this chapter on how to sit and the five key questions you should be able to answer. It is crucial you have good answers to them and can explain yourself fully to the interviewer(s).

Keep good eye contact throughout the interview and if there is more than one person interviewing you, then keep eye contact focus on the main interviewer first. Look them between the eyes, hold it for between 5–10 seconds and switch to number two and repeat throughout the interview. If there are more people you need to keep switching between them and not just address one person (unless they have asked you a specific question). Don't forget to **SMILE,** it changes how you speak.

Overcoming nerves

Having a job interview can be a daunting and pressure situation. Many people dread them and then wonder why they don't get the job. So the first thing you can do is get yourself into the right headspace for the interview. Arriving early and cooling down or warming up are essential firsts.

Always remember if a company invites you for an interview they must think you can do the job. Your covering letter and CV have shown them you have the experience and qualities they want. You now need to convince them you are the ideal candidate, so make sure you are prepared and have done the research about the job, the company, and the answers you want to give. If you're changing professions or moving to another sector, make sure you can sell your transferable skills to the new employer. Tell them how your experience in one sector can be used elsewhere.

Answering questions

Be ready with examples of answers you can give to different questions. Make sure you know what you are good at and be able to highlight that in the interview. So if you say you are good at conflict management or customer service have examples of this to talk about. Use the S.T.A.R technique to answer these questions.

Speak slowly and clearly and engage with the interviewer giving your answer the best you can. As I've mentioned before, practise your answers with others before the interview and iron out any issues you may have with them so that when you put on your performance in front of an employer it will be tried, tested and your very best.

Listen carefully to questions

Make sure you listen to what is being asked by the interviewer and understand what is wanted. If you don't know what is being looked for or you don't have an answer, you have three options:

1. *Repeat the question you've been asked back to them slowly (buying yourself time to think up an answer).*

2. *Ask them what they are looking for so you can clarify in your mind the answer you will give.*

3. *Ask if the question could be put to you another way.*

All these will buy you a little time to formulate an answer. If you really haven't got an answer you can say so but this might limit your chances of getting the job.

Life's a pitch

You are in front of these people to "pitch" yourself. It is the big prize and you have to want it enough to get it. Selling yourself is not always easy, as often we don't really know ourselves very well. You need to take time and think about yourself and the skills, experience and the personal qualities you have that you can offer the employer.

When people talk about selling they seem to glaze over and say, "oh I don't sell, I've never been good at it". We all sell ourselves every day to each other. If you are trying to convince somebody to do something or go somewhere then you are selling. If you want a child to behave or comply with your wishes, you are selling.

If you're in front of an employer you have to sell yourself, your skills, your abilities, your experience and personal qualities. So get used to pitching yourself.

If you're unemployed you should be out there selling yourself to anybody who'll listen (or not as the case may be). The more you do it, the better you will become. Practice makes perfect. Perform and refine your techniques often to ensure success.

After the interviewer has finished you may be asked if you have any questions. Make sure you have about three. You should avoid talking about holidays and the rate of pay at this stage. It is important to focus on training opportunities, promotion prospects and how the job role will develop over time. This will show you have an interest in the job and are thinking beyond the position now and are considering your future prospects.

Smile and be likeable

I've already mentioned this, but try to smile at the interview and always come across as likeable. When you smile you speak in a different tone. It is a sign of happiness and that will be reflected in the way you speak and come across to the employer. While I'm not saying you should make the interview a joke, you should nevertheless seem personable and have a sense of humour. Nobody wants to hire a cranky, sour-faced person. They want people who can be part of their team.

When it comes down to it, people are buying people. I often sit in front of clients who say they're qualified for the job but didn't get it. They think the world is against them. If you think like that, take a hard look at yourself. The biggest barrier you may be facing is yourself.

I once worked with a woman who was employed in local government and had been out of work for about two years. As is often the case, she was reluctantly on my course. She had worked in debt recovery and I suggested she look for work in debt collection. I reviewed her CV and did a mock interview with her. At the end I told her to make some changes to her CV and when she did interviews in the future to smile as in our mock one she was a little po-faced. Her immediate reaction was not good.

A week later she sent an email saying she went home, thought about what I'd said and revamped her CV and applied for two jobs. She was interviewed for both and offered one to start the following week. In her P.S. she added, "By the way, I smiled all the way through the interview". I'm always happy when I get a result like that.

Show interest

Whatever job you are applying for make sure you show you're interested in the company. Show you are keen on what they do. If you're in front of someone who started the company or runs it, it is their life's work so show enthusiasm for whatever is sold, manufactured or produced.

A company will expect you to know at least something about the organisation and what they do. This goes back to the research you do before the interview and should be an integral part of your pre-interview preparation. Showing interest and being enthusiastic could be the selling point that gets you the job. So always be aware you need to show that you are interested and enthusiastic about the company when sitting in front of a potential employer.

Give me a reason to employ you

At any interview a good answer to a question like this is key to getting a job. Even if you aren't asked it directly you should try and angle it so you can get your answer in. This is where you should go back to the exercise about writing down the ten things that tell someone everything about you. The answers you give should reflect you as a person and what you are all about.

The answer you give should be **MEMORABLE** and leave a **LASTING IMPRESSION** with the employer. When you leave the interview you have to be **REMEMBERED** by the interviewer. You have to **STAND OUT** from the competition and be the **OUTSTANDING** candidate. If you can't do that then someone before or after you will do it and get the job.

When you're in competition with so many other candidates you have to make sure you have done the best selling job to get yourself across compared to other interviewees. When you **STAND OUT** from the crowd what you give is your **USP** (Unique Selling Point). As individuals we are all unique so everyone has a USP. The employer has to buy into this and feel that you are the right person.

An employer is buying you, your time and experience to make money for their organisation. So individually you have to tick all the right boxes, be an ideal fit for the company and stand out from all the others who applied for the job. If you want to win think about how you will end your interview and leave the right impression to get hired.

Before you go

At the end of the interview thank the employers for interviewing you and find out when a decision about the job will be made. You could ask if there is anything else you could say to help them make their decision. Again, be ready with an answer that will be memorable.

Even if you are unsuccessful, you need to be able to get feedback on your performance so you can improve. This will help you hone your interview skills and do better next time.

Always remember to leave a good impression with the company. Even if you don't get the job you might be second on the list or they may consider you for another position or even recommend you for other roles they might have. You might even get the original job if the first candidate doesn't take it or proves to be unsuitable.

Summary

So these are the basics you have to be aware of when you attend interviews. It is all down to performance on the day and how you come across to employers. If they offer you an interview they believe you can do the job.

If you take that as a starting point you should not be nervous about the interview.

Once you are there your job is to convince them that you are the right candidate for the position. You are there to market yourself to them. Imagine you are a product and they are looking at the outside packaging when they see you. When you are asked questions they are unwrapping you to find out what's inside. They have to feel that what they are buying into is something they really want that will give them satisfaction, value and meet their needs. They need to be able to say at the end of the interview this person "does what it says on the tin" and meets all their requirements. If they can say that, they will be ready to buy. Also remember you are in competition with a lot of other products (people) who are also trying to do the same thing.

Your USP has to sell you to the potential employer and to give them a reason to hire you. At this point I'd suggest you review this chapter taking in all the points you need to succeed at interview. Each condition has to be satisfied if you are to succeed in getting a job. In today's market you have to be ready and prepared if you are serious about finding employment.

Getting a job in tough times is not impossible – just more difficult. The readier you are to meet the challenges, the greater chance you have of getting a job.

EXERCISE 5

1. Write down the answers you would give to the five key questions you know you could be asked at interview. Pay particular attention to question 3 about your strengths, question 4 about your weaknesses and question 5 about why a company should hire you.

2. Rehearse your answers with someone or practise them in the mirror. The more you do this, the better you will become. Your aim is to be as fluent and clear as possible so you can give yourself the best chance of getting the job.

3. Write answers to some of the random questions you may be asked. If you were a colour, what would you be and why? If you were an animal, what would you be and why? Be ready if you are asked similar questions.

4. Write yourself a script for a phone interview. What would you say? How would you sell yourself? Think about the speed and tone of your voice and how you sound on the phone. You can even record your answers and listen to them. It might be a bit frightening at first but that is how you sound to employers. If you don't like what you hear, work on improving it by practice.

5. If you do secure an interview, make sure you are fully prepared and ready so once you enter the room you can relax and give the best performance and get the job.

CHAPTER EIGHT

To Be Hired or Not To Be Hired? That is the Question

If you don't get the job, then take heart. You are not alone. The competition for positions is fierce and you will have been up against a lot of well-qualified candidates. You should be proud of the fact you managed to get an interview and you were close to getting a job. *FEEDBACK* is now key.

Once you know the reasons why you didn't get the job you need to review what went well and what could be improved. As I mentioned earlier a big part of getting the job is the performance you give at the interview. You need to find out what can be done better if you are to succeed next time. Don't look at it as failure but see it as positive feedback. It is something you can learn from to help develop yourself further to guarantee success in the future.

Take the feedback and use it to change your techniques. Refine areas which need improvement and eradicate what went wrong. By doing this you can make sure you don't make the same mistakes in the future. Once you have made the necessary changes, practise them to ensure you get it right at the next interview.

Remember what I said about performance; if you want to get it right then practise it often. The more you practise the better you will get at it. They say repetition is the master of skill, so keep working to improve your interview techniques.

Don't take feedback from employers in a negative way, and don't get involved in arguments with those giving the feedback. Remember they are giving you advice on what went wrong in their eyes and how you could do better next time. It could be that you were extremely close and might be considered for other positions.

It's not easy but keep trying

A key part of job hunting is to be persistent. This is where most people fail. They think that after being rejected a few times they have no chance of getting a job, they fall into a spiral of negativity and they believe they are unemployable. Older people talk about ageism and being passed over for younger candidates. I have to say that while I think this is true in some cases, it does not mean there are no opportunities out there. I've actually found it to be a positive; age does have benefits.

Speaking as a 56-year-old disabled person (with a severe walking disability) I have found work and continue to do so. That has more to do with my desire to keep working and being told that I can't do something. In the last case I left a job because I hated the employer and had difficulty getting to and from the offices. My wife's comment was (given my age and physical condition) "you'll never work again".

It is strange that a few months later I saw an advert online and applied for work to train the long-term unemployed at a local college. I think she was highly surprised when I was hired. My key piece of advice is if you want job keep applying and working at it and work will follow.

Get in front of the right people

It is most important to keep trying to get yourself in front of the people who make decisions about hiring staff. Find out who they are and make a concerted effort to speak to them. Ring, write or find a way to contact them and ask them for the chance to come and talk about potential work opportunities. Don't ask for a job but use it to find out about the business or industry and sell yourself.

You need to ensure you engage with the right people in organisations. HR departments tend only to fill positions and have little real authority. You need to find the boss or head of the organisation to have real impact. It is he or she who ultimately decides who is taken on and this is the person you need to get in front of.

When you talk to them find out if there are or are going to be any opportunities either with them or anybody they know. It does help if you have an idea about what you want to do (I refer to earlier in the book where I talked about clarity and focus) and see if you can make an opportunity for yourself. If they see potential they might create a position for you.

An example of this concerns my older son who, after graduating, was looking to start a career in the recruitment industry. Despite applying for jobs and being interviewed he was not getting a break. We knew somebody who ran a small recruitment agency and convinced him to talk to her. After a phone call and a meeting she created a position in her business because she saw his potential and gave him his first job.

Talk to those who might help

As well as persistence, keep talking to people about what you are looking for. You have to keep telling yourself you will find a job. It might not be quite what you wanted but it has to be a starting point to get you back on your feet.

Embrace every meeting and tell others that you are looking for work. Ask them if they know anybody who could help you. Networking is now a vital part of the job-hunting process and is the best way to find work.

As I mentioned before only about 20% of the available jobs are advertised. Around 80% of jobs are filled by people recommended by staff already working there, so always keep up your network of contacts and people you can talk to about work possibilities.

You should also talk to people you meet. They might have a vital piece of information to help you look in the right direction. There are two examples from my own family about how talking to people got them a break.

My mother came to the UK in the 1950s having been a teacher trainer in her native India. On arriving in Britain she found it extremely difficult to find work. She had written off for dozens of jobs but to no avail. One day she was sitting at an underground station in London and got into conversation with a young woman. It turned out they were both teachers, so my mum asked if she knew of any job opportunities. The woman told her that a borough in East London was urgently looking for teachers. She bought a ticket and travelled across London and went straight into the local town hall. She was snapped up immediately and started work the next day.

More recently my mother-in-law was made redundant from her job in the shipping industry. At 64 she thought there was no hope of getting work. One day she was in our local shopping centre and saw a new shop that sold items from the past. Intrigued she walked in and was immediately caught up in a sense of nostalgia. A few minutes later she talked with the man inside the shop telling him how much she liked it. The conversation got round to her redundancy when the man suddenly said, "I'm looking for a part-time member of staff; would you be interested?" She jumped at the chance and was back in work again.

So you see sometimes engaging in conversation with people can have a major impact on your job opportunities.

You never know who you're talking to

I'm adding this section as it's important to remember that wherever you are and whoever you speak to may be a potential employer. A good friend of mine works in the shipping industry and is always on the lookout for excellent customer service staff. On one occasion she was in her local supermarket and she engaged in conversation with a young woman working on the tills. Having been impressed by her she found out a bit about her background and discovered she wanted more than to work on a supermarket checkout. Before my friend left she handed over her business card and told the young woman to contact her.

On another occasion she took her car in to be serviced. There was pandemonium at the garage but a young man behind the counter dealt exclusively with her making sure her needs were met and that everything was in order. When she returned at the end of the day there was a similar situation but this one young man appeared cool, calm and collected throughout. She asked him a few questions about his ambitions and gave him her business card to contact her. Needless to say both these people were employed by her, and she says they are the best employees she has ever taken on.

Always remember that the impression you create and the way you engage with people can have a major impact on your chances of finding work. Sometimes the way you interact and deal with those you come into contact with and the impression you create could lead to your being offered work.

Look outside your normal area

I have mentioned this before but if you find there are few opportunities in the places you used to work, then look further afield. Be prepared to find work outside your normal remit area. It is much like the fishing analogy; if you were trying to catch fish and you got nothing, the best strategy would be to try elsewhere.

It's the same with work. Look somewhere else and find out where there are opportunities and go there.

While this may put you out and be more expensive, the important thing is to get working. Once you do this you have momentum and your life will start moving in a different direction. From there you can start looking for other opportunities. It is always better to be working and looking for a job than not working and seeking employment. In the eyes of the employer you are perceived as a much more credible candidate if you are in work and have a working history.

Do the unusual and get noticed

In today's market it is vital you **STAND OUT** from the crowd. Being noticed is a key part of the job-hunting process. With companies receiving hundreds or even thousands of CVs, you really have to make an **IMPRESSION** if you want to be noticed.

Some people have gone to extraordinary lengths to get work. They've ranged from standing out on a roundabout with a board and a number, being out in freezing conditions handing out leaflets or even setting up websites and selling themselves on eBay to get a job.

Sometimes you have to be creative or use lateral thinking if you are determined to land a job. There can be no half measures for serious job hunters. Think about how you can get in front of those with influence who hire people. Identify them and find a way to arrange a meeting or the chance to talk to them personally.

This is where your desire to find a job will come into play. You will need to be committed to the process and prepared to convince potential employers you are the right candidate.

If you are prepared to chance your luck you might be in the right place at the right time to get taken on. As I mentioned previously, most jobs are taken before they're advertised and getting in front of an employer at a crucial time (when they have a need to find somebody in a hurry) may mean you get the job with little or no real competition. Remember you are trying to get someone's attention and to do something which will make employers take notice of you.

Job-hunting may not be easy, but it's not impossible. You have to stalk a job a bit like a hunter and use all your skill, guile and experience to snare it. Once you have it, it's important you do everything to keep it, which I'll cover in the next chapter.

CHAPTER NINE

You're Hired, Now Prove You're the Right Person for the Job

Getting a job is the first part of joining a new organisation or company and you need to be ready for the challenges ahead. Most people think that having got the job they can relax. It's here the real work begins and you need to get into a regular pattern to ensure you do well and keep the job you've worked so hard to get.

Get into a Good Routine

If you've been out of work for some time you need to get back into some good habits. Make sure you get a good night's sleep and rest well. There is nothing worse than starting a job being late and feeling tired. Think about the impression that is creating with your employer and new fellow employees.

You could also think about getting yourself fit and eating better. Your body and mind are like a muscle. They need to be fed, nourished and exercised to work properly. If you start abusing yourself you will pay the price (if not now then eventually). You need to use your body and mind on a regular basis. The more you do it, the stronger and fitter you will become.

Adapt to all things new

Remember you are going to have to adapt to new people, places and situations. At first these will seem strange to you and you have to think about how and where you will fit into the organisation. There may be a certain culture and method you have to get used to and also new ways of working. You may need to change your outlook and view of the world based on the new surroundings.

It's important that you embrace the changes that will occur in your life and adapt to them quickly. These days, employers usually have a probation period where you both see if you can work together. It's a bit like marriage, only they can divorce you without too much hassle and not have to pay you an arm and a leg to do it.

The important thing is to fit into the organisation and feel like you're part of it and that you are contributing to future success. Employers are increasingly looking for this and how much value you are bringing to their organisation. The more you bring, the more valued you become and the more you can earn.

Meet challenges head on

Every new job brings a set of new challenges. It's important you identify these in your new role and learn to meet them. If you are struggling with them then ask for help.

All too often you come across a problem when joining a new organisation and then either fail or mess up. I speak from my own experience here and I should have asked for help and support to ensure it all worked out. Don't struggle in silence; get the help you need to meet the expectations of your employer. If you have a major issue, raise it with your line manager.

Your aim is to seek support and help at what is a critical time for your long-term job prospects. Dealing with issues now may mean you keep the job and grow and develop in the company rather than being sacked or let go.

Good and bad days

Not every day at work is going to be great and we all have bad days at the office. It is important to understand this and to make sure you don't let the bad days get to you. A lot of this is to do with the way you approach issues at work. There are those who take their work problems home and this can have a disastrous effect on their home life. It's important you understand that any issues you have in the workplace should be resolved there.

Don't expect it to all go smoothly; there may be problems. You should be prepared to deal with these issues when they occur and to face them head on. Do not suffer in silence and make sure you get your colleagues and managers to help resolve the problem before it goes too far and affects your personal and professional life.

If it gets too much and things are not working out, then maybe the position isn't for you. It's important then to plan what to do next.

The job's not for me

Not every job will work out. Sometimes there is a total mismatch and the position, company and you are all at odds with one another. It's important you identify this at an early stage. It would also help if you can discuss your concerns with your employer, but this isn't always possible.

If you decide you are going to leave a job, make sure you do so on good terms. You shouldn't just not turn up or go without saying anything. If you feel the job is not for you, speak to the HR department or your boss. Explain your position and what you want to do. See if there are other opportunities within the organisation that you could move into as you are already employed by the company.

If it's taken you some time to find this position then you might have difficulty trying to find another job. This may mean going through the whole process again to find a new opportunity. You might wish to stay in the position until you find something else but the important thing is to make sure you do not leave a job on bad terms.

If you do apply for another job, you will probably have to give your current employer as a reference and it's vital you have performed well enough to be given a good one. There's nothing worse than falling out with an employer and then struggling to find another job without having a good reference.

Make sure you have done everything within your power to make a good impression with your employer, and that you have worked to your best ability in the job. The overall aim is to have done enough to ensure your exit from the company is smooth and you can move into another job with your reputation intact.

While in the UK technically you can't be given a bad reference and employers are wary of doing so for fear of legal action against them if they're not 100 per cent accurate. But if you get a neutral or OK one it says a lot about you to any potential employer. The last thing you want is to set alarm bells ringing before you even get offered a new job. Therefore ensure you've done everything you can to make the transition between jobs as pain free as possible.

Keep the job until you get another

Despite having reservations or concerns about your current job, you might want to start looking for work whilst you still have it. Other employers will be more inclined to take on those who are in work than those who are not.

It's always important to understand that if you are working your employer has decided you are employable. People assume that the reason they don't get a job is because they did something wrong at the interview. Often it's to do with how you are perceived by the employer and if they think you are the right fit to work as part of the company.

If you've been unemployed for some time, employers have little to measure you by or to ascertain if you can work as part of their team. If you are in work then you have a track record and this will bode well for you. Being in work has a lot of benefits and generates the right impression to future employers.

Always remember that you should leave on good terms and not become involved in arguments about the job. The cleaner and more amicable the break, the better for all concerned. Instead of getting angry and resentful focus your mind on moving forward and getting back into work as soon as possible.

CHAPTER TEN

Do Something Different:
Retraining for the Future

If you are facing unemployment and feel it would be difficult for you to find similar work in your field you could always look at retraining or doing something completely different, I've found this myself in my own working life. For most of my career I worked in radio and television news as a reporter, producer, presenter and programme editor. In 2009 I was made redundant after a contract I was working on ended. When my job finished, I decided I wasn't going to work in the media any more. It had become a young person's game and at 50, with 22 years in the business, I felt it was time to do something different.

Luckily for me I had the foresight to predict this the year before and I was prepared. I'd already studied Neuro-Linguistic Programming (I'm a Master Practitioner) and from 2008 I also became a Certified Business and Life Coach. While I was building my coaching business (which was quite tough) I undertook some business development work.

In December 2010 out of the blue I received a phone call from my sister-in-law asking if I'd be interested in training the long-term unemployed as they were desperate for trainers (a clear example of someone I know getting me into an unknown sector). I ended up doing it for a few weeks and went back to work for them a few months later. I think I found a bit of a niche where all my training and coaching expertise could be used.

As I told you earlier, I needed a PTTLS (Preparing to Teach in the Lifelong Sector) teaching qualification, which I didn't have. My employer paid for it and I did it on the firm's time. When I joined another company they said I needed IAG (Information Advice and Guidance), which they paid for and I became qualified in that as well.

Since moving into this field I have developed a number of new skills that I have successfully used with various training organisations to help the long-term unemployed.

Think about what you want to do

If you are thinking of undertaking any training I suggest you do some research into what people are looking for, the kind of service they want and the price they will pay for it. This is vitally important, as there are thousands of courses that you can undertake and just as many training companies only too willing relieve you of your hard earned cash. Even if your employer is paying for it (as part of your redundancy package) the choice you make here is vital if you are going to succeed in your chosen field.

Reputable training organisation

Make sure the training provider is reputable and has a record of getting or helping students to get work after their course. There is nothing worse than completing your training only to find nobody will use you (especially if you have no experience!).

The most notable one in the UK is security training. The courses are fine as is getting the badge to show you're licenced to do the job. The only problem is that many employers (and agencies who handle the work) only want those with experience, so for many it's a Catch 22 situation; with no experience there's no work.

Be aware of what you are doing and why

If you are contemplating undertaking training, plan what you are going to do with it. It would be better if you spoke to those working in the field you want to go into and asked about where the work opportunities are. That way you can tailor your training to potential jobs.

As I've said before, don't undertake anything that will not provide you with opportunities. Know in advance what you want to do, plan what you will do with your training and then take steps in that direction.

Being market or job savvy is crucial at this stage. The last thing you want is to have spent hard earned money only to find there are no real opportunities. There's nothing wrong with learning new skills as long as you can utilise them to help you earn money.

It's the same with university degrees. Some graduates complete their course and expect there to be work out there. Just having a degree means almost nothing. It's just an entry ticket to the jobs market. In my day only ten per cent of the UK population had a degree, now almost forty per cent have one. They have become devalued in the eyes of employers; they now want more. There are jobs, but employers want the best candidates. They seek people who have an idea about what they want to do and have taken steps to get some experience in that field. The graduate who has done this and has a plan is much more likely to find work.

It's also the same for those seeking training in new fields hoping to change career. Know what you want to do, be clear about what you need to do to get there and follow a plan to achieve it.

Be aware it might not always be plain sailing and things may go wrong along the way but achieving goals and being flexible in what you do will certainly help you get there. Planning to succeed is crucial. It's not what you've got, it's how you use it that counts. Your qualifications and training are just part of the big picture of what you will need, being aware of this is very important in order to be successful.

CHAPTER ELEVEN

Creating a Job
for Yourself

In the Great Britain it's becoming increasingly clear the UK government is looking to extend the working life of individuals. As I write the state pension age has risen from 65 to up to 67 years depending on when you were born. That might go higher as time goes on. The old traditional days of working for the same company all your life and ending work with a gold watch or clock at 65 are well and truly numbered. In reality you are going to have to work longer and probably harder before you are considered too old and ready for retirement.

If finding work has become difficult (and that's despite there being laws about ageism and people being told to take on older workers) you need to consider what else you can do to make money and earn a living. Often, I have people in front of me during my training sessions who complain about the lack of jobs, work being given to the young or taken by migrants coming to the UK. There are probably cases where this is true, but a lot where it isn't.

Many people never think about what else they can do. I've had plasterers, builders, cake makers, clothes designers, web designers, and those who volunteer to do good works. Others have some great hobbies and skills that they could use to make money yet they fail to recognise opportunities.

In today's consumer society people want all types of services. They are essentially lazy and want it all done for them. They expect employers to have work. They want the government to pay them benefits if they are not working. In terms of their personal lives they are looking for convenience. They want others to do it and then to get the benefits by simply paying for it.

I recently had a former car wash owner on my course, who was looking for work after his site was closed down. He told me they were taking £1000 a day as a minimum in cash with very little outlay. In a year that's over £350,000. Even after his costs, there is still money to be made. If people are too lazy to wash their cars, what else don't they want to do? What are they prepared to pay for?

Older people are also looking for services. An ageing society will always need people to do work, think about it; gardening, house cleaning, DIY, painting and decorating, shopping – the list is endless. People are always looking for services that mean they don't have to do it themselves. This is how you can start your own business.

There are some important things you should do before you go down this route.

Get good-quality information

Always be on the lookout for where people have problems. That can be anything from queuing to buy products to spotting that people have an overgrown garden. Ask people if they are looking for any type of product or service that you could provide. At this stage it doesn't matter what it is, you are just gathering information. The aim is to find a common theme of what people want and what they are prepared to pay for it. Once you have this, start providing them with what they want.

Why this is so important

Do you ever see new businesses open up in your local area and then disappear a few months later? Have you ever wondered why? Many people dream of running their own business and often plough all their savings into it without thinking it through first. They open for business in hope and anticipation. When it doesn't work out they shut up shop and do something else and they are considerably poorer than when they started the business.

If only they'd asked people what they wanted before they invested their hard-earned cash. Finding out what people want is crucial for business success. Supermarkets do it all the time; if you have a loyalty card you are giving them information. They know what you buy, when and where you buy it, and how much you are spending. They give you loyalty points (to exchange for goods) and you give them information. They can then use this information to target you with products and services.

Never has the saying "information is power" been so appropriate. This is exactly what you need to do. Finding out what people want and are prepared to pay for is vital to business success. When you know what people want, give it to them.

From small acorns

Start doing things on a small scale and see whether it works. Can you make any money at it? You could even do a couple of jobs for free just to get yourself started as long as the people you do it for will give you a testimonial and recommend you to others. Sometimes you have to give something to get something back. Remember you are not doing a job for free – you are getting a recommendation and a testimonial to get yourself more work and develop a new business.

Build on this start

It's from here you want to be building your reputation in whatever area you want to run a business. In truth it is how you sell yourself to people that will determine your success. Also important is your ability to undertake different jobs for different people.

If you do painting and decorating, for example, you will often find people offering you other work. Once you have done something for them they start to trust you and will often ask if you could do other jobs for them. Often they won't even ask you how much you charge and they are only too happy to pay you.

It goes back to the pleasure and pain principle; if something is causing them pain and you can solve it for them then they will be happy and get pleasure from not having to deal with it themselves.

Developing things further

You now have the start of a small business which you've generated yourself. The beauty of this is that you are your **OWN BOSS.** You are now in charge of your own destiny with no one telling you what to do. All you have to do is keep your customers happy and convince others to use your service. This is how to begin to build a small business. It doesn't have to be huge and can actually be a micro-business giving you the earning potential so you don't have to look for a job.

EXERCISE 6

1. Think about and write down the skills or interests you have that could be sold as a service to others. At this stage it could be anything. Just get your thoughts down on paper and review them.

2. Look around for an opportunity and find out what drives you and others nuts with frustration and anger. Could you do it better? How would it differ from what's currently available? Did you know if you did something just 10% better than the competition you could become seriously wealthy? Something as small as this could have real bearing on what you might be able to do in the future.

3. Ask 100 people what problems they have with different products and services and what they would like to happen. Can you see a service or something you could provide them? Ask them how often they'd need it and what they would pay for it.

4. Start doing it on a small scale; the aim is to see if it is viable. You might even offer to do it for free to build a good reputation and trust with your customers. This should be your first building block and give you the step up you need to establish a business.

5. Ask your first customers to recommend you to others. Any businessman will tell you the

best business is that which comes from a recommendation. Also while you're working somewhere knock on doors and offer your services to see if you can drum up any business.

6. If this all goes to plan you have a fledgling business that you can grow and develop over time. This might not be easy to start with but it's what you build from these steps that will help take you in the right direction and hopefully lead to success.

NOTE If you are going down this path make sure you decide when, as you will have to inform people of what you're doing. You will need to become self-employed and tell the relevant authorities, notably the tax office, that you are now running a business. Before you start you should also do a business startup course. In the UK there are a lot of government paid for business courses to guide you on how to set up and run your own business. You should attend one and find out what it's like to be working for yourself and what you need to do to start in business.

Running your own business is not brain surgery and just about anybody can do it. However, it is very different from working for somebody and it will take a different attitude and mindset if you are to be successful. Just like a job there will be good and bad days and you will always be solving problems. You will also have to be highly motivated and driven to achieve success even when things don't look like they're going well. But if you get it right the rewards are high and you will have created something that will pay you for many years to come.

CHAPTER TWELVE

Working in the 21st Century

In today's working world you have to be prepared for change and maybe being made redundant from work some time in your career. It's the way of the modern world. For those of us who came from a different generation where people worked for one employer for life and retired with a gold watch thirty-five or forty years later, we have to accept that those days have sadly gone forever. In the high-tech fast-paced world of today you have to be constantly updating your skills and you have to be ready to embrace changes that are occurring in the workplace.

Many low-paid skilled jobs in the UK now require you to have qualifications. Building site workers must now hold a CSCS (Construction Site Certification Scheme) card, those working in the care industry must have an

NVQ in social care, to drive a forklift truck you need a licence with reach and counterbalance, and to work in security you have to have an SIA licence.

Inevitably this has led to a growth in the training sector and there are lots of opportunities there (I should know; I work in that sector). So if you are working in a particular field make sure you keep up to date with developments and changes that are taking place. Consider undertaking any training that's required and update your skills on a regular basis.

You may also find that in an increasingly competitive market employers are raising the bar and wanting higher qualifications and greater experience before they employ people. So if you decide to change career and undertake a training course you may find it difficult to break into a new sector as you have no relevant experience.

So, how do you change careers? What steps do you need to take to make it in a new field? And is it possible to make those changes later in life?

Use contacts and resources available to you to get working

Whatever field you want to go into you will need a helping hand. You need somebody prepared to give you an opportunity to show what you can do. On a personal level this happened to me. After a successful career in the media I decided to change direction and move into coaching, education and training at the age of 51.

Prior to leaving the media I had undertaken some training at my own cost to help me build a different career. As I mentioned earlier, my sister-in-law got me into the training sector. The firm was desperate and took a leap of faith to employ me with little or no experience. Once I was given the chance to show what I could do I became a trainer of the long-term unemployed.

I spent two weeks working there and gained some valuable experience on which I could build. I was also able to impress them enough to get a reference for other employers and to be considered for any future vacancies. That experience became invaluable and was the platform I needed to get my next job doing the same work with other companies before eventually developing a career in this sector.

There's always a price to pay

The biggest issue facing most people when looking for work today is what salary they're prepared to accept. With so many people looking for work employers are paying much less. In my case to change profession I took a 50% pay cut; it is the price I had to pay in order to do something completely different.

Whatever field you are in or are going into, employers simply don't have to pay as much as they used to. With a ready pool of people willing to work there are never any shortages of potential staff.

If you want a salary that is too high, then companies might go for the cheaper option, so be prepared to take a pay cut to get yourself working. Once you get into an industry or sector find out which areas are growing and paying more money and try to move into those. Also make yourself indispensable so that employers become dependent on you and have to employ and keep you because they have a need.

Get into a position of scarcity

In the world of work having the skills companies need is an important way of making you more employable. If you have something that is in short supply you will find work and people will pay you handsomely for your skills.

Think about it; if you need surgery or someone to play professional football, there is only a limited number of people who can do that kind of work. Because of this, these people are paid a **PREMIUM** for their services. There are other trades-people who may do the same job, but get paid considerably less. If you want to earn more money, you have to have a niche or a skill that is in demand.

If you can position yourself in a market or job and have skills that are needed you will always be able to command a higher salary and be constantly employed. It really is a case of less is more; the scarcer your skills, the more demand you create.

Two such professions that come to mind are chimney sweeps and thatchers. In the first instance you may have a vision of Dick Van Dyke in Mary Poppins, but the reality is that while most homes are now centrally heated, real fires are back in fashion. So there are fewer chimney sweeps, but they are in demand and command a higher price. Thatchers put straw roofs on ancient buildings in the UK and while homes now tend to have tiled roofs, those with thatched roofs still need repairs. This puts thatchers in a premium position and they are paid well for their skills.

Become invaluable to an organisation

Whatever you do and wherever you work, make yourself invaluable to an organisation. Be prepared to do what others won't do. Always go the extra mile and take on additional responsibilities. Getting into this position will almost always guarantee you don't lose your job.

When people become reliant on you they always ask you to do more. They trust you and will call on you to help out in other areas. Even if you have not done it before be ready to take on the challenge. The more you can do, the more useful you become to the company you work for. Don't get caught up in the "it's not my job" syndrome.

Every experience you have in employment is something you can add to your CV and ensure you keep working. Use this platform to get employers to train you and boost your skills and qualifications.

Get training paid for by the employer

With the growing demand for well-qualified employees companies are demanding their staff have CPD (Continuing Personal Development). This ensures that workers keep their skills up to date and can use these in the job. So it is in the interests of organisations to offer ongoing training.

It is also often in the interests of an employer to have well trained staff who can undertake a number of different roles. Training is the key to this. It is always worth asking employers if they will pay for training, you would then develop skills which can be used in their workplace.

From my own personal experience, which I've already mentioned, employers need to have well qualified staff and are often prepared to pay for it. Two recent examples of training I've received are first aid and food hygiene. The first was for use in the workplace and the second was because I had to teach it. Both are now things I can put on my CV as an aid to find work and to show my commitment to CPD.

Be aware of what's happening in your sector

Even if you've been in a job many years, never rest on your laurels. Always be conscious of changes and the impact they could have on your job prospects. If at any time you feel uncertainty, start looking around at other options.

Think about what else you could do. Can you have training outside work that may help you change your career? What contacts do you have if you have to find another job? Is your CV up to date and ready to send out?

Being continuously employed in tough times is about anticipation and preparation. If you know what is going on with your job, company or industry and you are ready for any changes, then the chances are you will be able to adjust and keep working. Don't bury your head in the sand and ignore changes that are happening around you.

Network with those who can help you

Whatever your situation always make sure you network and meet people who might be able to assist you in finding work. If you want to enter a new field think about who might be able to offer guidance and support to get you there. Ask people for help.

As adults it's often hard to ask people to help as we think we don't need it or can do without it. If you are facing unemployment or redundancy then it is important you get as much help as you can. Don't just ask for a job, talk to people about what you want to do and find out what you would need to achieve it.

Is there anything you could be doing such as education, training or work experience? Where are the opportunities in your chosen sector? How would you qualify and what chance do you stand of getting the job against experienced candidates? Who else can you speak to about finding work? The aim is to build up a body of information you can use to steer your way into employment.

The most difficult part is asking for help. Once you've overcome this the rest is straightforward. The more people you can engage in helping you, the better chance you have of finding work.

This process has a dual effect. It conveys the message that you are looking for work and it reinforces in your mind that you are doing something productive to find a job.

Do something unusual and get noticed

In today's jobs market it is vital to get noticed. You have to stand out from the crowd. Simply sending off CVs and writing letters may not get you the results you want. That might inspire you to think out of the box.

Many people have taken unusual methods to get noticed. People have been known to stand with "give me a job" placards or billboards. You could stand at a roundabout or busy junction or a station handing out flyers, or you could go in to companies asking for any opportunities. You can come up with your own ideas to become visible to employers.

If you are serious about finding work, do something that makes you stand out from others. Show you have the skills to be different and impress an employer to hire you.

Become a portfolio worker

With the change in the way we work now affecting more of us (and that includes me) you might consider becoming a "portfolio worker". That means you may do two or even three different jobs rather than seeking one line of employment. This might not suit everybody, but if you are not averse to a degree of uncertainty and don't mind chopping and changing professions, then portfolio working may be for you.

I have been in this position for many years. During my time working in the media, I spent most of it as a freelance producer. During one period I was working exclusively for one employer for 18 months. On a wet Tuesday afternoon he took me outside and said, "I'm expanding my business but using your salary to do it, so here's your last pay cheque".

It couldn't have come at a worse time, as a number of new media operations were also shutting down making competition for freelance work extremely tough. To make ends meet I started working as a private hire driver slotting in media work when it came up. I also made a decision to start a franchise cleaning business so I wouldn't be relying on one source of income.

I have to admit I did take a huge gamble and re-mortgaged my house to finance the business. Luckily this has paid off and I am still running it now. During this period a new job opportunity also arose which I took and stayed with for eight years. I continued to run my business in line with whatever else I was doing.

While working in the media I also realised I wanted to change what I was doing and I undertook a number of different personal development courses that paved the way to future work opportunities. These skills have been vital in helping me boost my career prospects.

When I was made redundant in 2009 I made a commitment to myself not to work in the media as I was tired of it and it had become a young person's industry. I found some part-time work in business development and began my coaching business as well as continuing to run my cleaning franchise.

I was then offered the chance to train the long-term unemployed which I am doing as well as undertaking my other business activities. So you see you can do a number of different jobs at the same time if you are flexible, can think on your feet and deal with constant change. It certainly makes for a more interesting working life and allows you to use a wide range of skills.

As I said before, this is not for everybody and the thought of constantly changing roles and positions doesn't sit well with people who like continuity. For others, though, it might provide the flexibility to work on different projects or different jobs. This not only gives them a good living but also has more job satisfaction than any one position would give. It's just another option to think about if you are serious about finding work.

Agencies, short-term and long-term contract work

In employment terms, many companies have realised they don't need people all the time. They might need to hire help on a short-term or long-term basis. While they might do this themselves, many go through agencies that vet and supply staff for various projects. From a working perspective, this could provide you with short-term opportunities.

You can undertake these on a regular basis and this can lead to a permanent position. This doesn't just apply to jobs requiring a low level of skill, but also to many firms including banks, lawyers and local authorities. A lot of jobs will be like this in the future.

If you go through an agency they will generally only call you if they have a need. The rest of the time you might not hear from them. Don't take this personally as they tend to work on a "needs" requirement and that will depend on market demand. If you do go through agencies, sign up with more than one. Keep in contact with them on a regular basis and build relationships with consultants who can put work your way when it comes in.

You will also need to be flexible in terms of when, where and how you work and be prepared to fit in with the requirements of the job. Again, when you are working somewhere make yourself invaluable and talk to those there about opportunities within the company. This is a key way of identifying potential jobs from the inside.

Zero-hour contracts

There's a lot of debate about these contracts where companies sign you up and offer you work when they have it. For some people this works out well but for others there have been horror stories about being tied in with one company and not being able to work elsewhere even if your contractor has no work.

As I write, the UK government is consulting industry about this exclusivity and whether it should be outlawed. The rule here is therefore simple. If you are being asked to sign a zero-hour contract make sure it isn't exclusive and that you can work elsewhere if they have no hours to offer you.

A key part of this type of working is that it can come at any time and you have to be flexible and adaptable in terms of both times and the type of work you do. From the employer's perspective the more flexible you are the better and if you can constantly show you are available for work, the more chance you have of being called on a regular basis.

Zero-hour contracts are becoming a popular way of hiring staff on a short-term basis and you should be aware of them as they represent another avenue you can pursue in your quest to find work. It may be that it fits in with your lifestyle or requirements and you can work this way indefinitely. Again, this is a reality of 21st century working you need to know about and you can embrace it as part of your employment journey.

Summary

So, these are a few things you could do to get yourself employed in the 21st century. There is a whole host of others and these are just the tip of the iceberg. How you get working and what you do is up to you. It all comes down to what you are prepared to do to get a job. In the final chapter, I'll give you some thoughts on how you can take charge of your life and get yourself working.

CHAPTER THIRTEEN

Getting a Job:

Take Action,
The Power is in Your Hands

I find many people who are unemployed put themselves in the hands of others. In the UK you can get benefits and you are at the mercy of the job centre, which dictates what you can get and what you have to do to get it. The unemployed are often put on courses or programmes that are supposed to help them find work but they have limited success. If they don't do them their benefit money is sanctioned.

In this position you may feel powerless and that your life is out of control. You may get angry and frustrated at the system and what's happening in the economy. There is always someone else to blame for your predicament.

My advice is to take a long hard look at yourself and think why you are unemployed. Are you simply hoping a job will come along like the 23 bus? Or do you want a job handed to you on a plate? In my view the biggest problem facing the unemployed today is staring them in the mirror – **THEMSELVES!**

Where you are today is a reflection of the decisions or choices you made in the past. Most of your life you've played by certain rules, which have worked. Now they've stopped working. Unfortunately, you are still trying to use those strategies and are expecting a different outcome. That's madness! It just won't happen.

If you want something different to happen, change yourself and what you are doing. By shaking things up you will get a different outcome. It could be as simple as changing your cover letter or CV. You might like to talk to somebody about what you want to do or change the way you look.

A key point here is to not stop once you have made the changes. You may still be annoyed and frustrated as people will always put barriers and obstacles in front of you. In today's world the word "no" is a natural response to most things. You will also hear "you can't do that" because you are too old, too inexperienced, or lack the right qualifications.

Your job is to convince employers you are the right person for the job and that they should give you an opportunity to show them what you can do. You can even offer to do a few days for free. Remember what

I've said before; give something to get something back. If you do any work you should at least get a reference or a recommendation.

Under these circumstances, you are going to get a lot of nos, but the key thing is to keep going until you succeed. Many adults seem to stop trying if they get a few nos. However, if you think back to when you were a child and learnt how to walk, how many times did you fall over? Did you just sit there and cry? No – you got up and did it again and again and again until you perfected it. It's the same with getting a job in tough times.

If you want to succeed you have to be persistent. Keep going until you achieve what you want. Don't give up until you get a job. If people put up barriers (and they will) or say "no", find another way to do it. Successful people are those who are prepared to do what others won't do to get what they want.

The truth is your future is in your own hands. I'm not in charge of your destiny and the only person who is is **YOU**. It is the action you take, the determination you have and your desire to find work that will get you what you want.

It is hard to get yourself a job in the current economic climate, but it's not impossible. I hope this book has given you food for thought, inspiration and some ideas about how to find a job in tough times.

I wish you every success in your hunt for work and I hope that the strategies and methods in this book have given you ideas about what you need to do to get yourself working. Never believe you are unemployable or there are no jobs out there. Where there are people living together in any area they are always looking for products and services; if that's the case then there must be jobs. Your task is to tap into your inner potential and find out what people want and give it to them. It doesn't matter what's going on in the economy. If you can do that as either a supplier or worker in any field you are sure to keep yourself in work.

The Final Word

Thank you for taking the time to read this book and I hope you now have some real strategies to get your first job or get yourself back into work. I know they work because I have been successful using them with the long-term unemployed in the UK. Those who I have worked with and who have taken my advice have seen positive results. I hope the same happens for you.

For more information about finding the perfect job in tough times please go to my blog/website **www. thejobhuntingtookit.com**. I'll be adding regular updates on how you can get working and new tips and strategies to help get a job you really want.

I am always keen to hear about your experiences and what works for you. You can leave comments there or contact me at **oni.b1958@gmail.com**. If there is anything you want me to add please let me know or if there are issues you'd like help with I'll try to do that through my website.

Thank you again for reading. As always, it's been an honour, privilege and pleasure sharing this information with you and I hope to do more of the same in the future.

Oni Bhattacharya

About the Author

Oni Bhattacharya is a leading Employability Trainer in the UK who has worked in both the private and public sector with the long-term unemployed. He developed his ideas working in this field bringing together life coaching skills, a no-nonsense approach and practical ways to get working fast. As well as being a qualified business and life coach he is a Master Practitioner of NLP (Neuro-Linguistic Programming), which he uses in his work. Before entering this field he spent 22 years as a TV and radio news producer, presenter, editor and reporter, working for most of the UK's leading broadcasters. He also runs a contract cleaning franchise and has worked in retailing and customer service. He has been married for 25 years, has two sons and currently lives in Essex.

ABOUT THE AUTHOR

Lightning Source UK Ltd.
Milton Keynes UK
UKOW06f1846300415

250694UK00007B/72/P